# Engage.
# Lead.
# Deliver.

*Leadership Tenets for Tapping into the Collective Genius of Your People*

## DARYLL BRYANT

PUBLISHED BY BLUE ARTISTS, LLC

# CONTENTS

# FOREWORD

As a 1965 graduate of the U.S. Military Academy at West Point, I was given significant leadership responsibility right out of college, leading a platoon in combat in Vietnam. After 13 years of service in the U.S. Army, I joined General Motors Corporation as a manufacturing executive, operating business units with as many as 7,000 employees and one billion dollars in revenue. Following General Motors, over the last 25 years I have acquired some 15 companies with a combined revenue, at one point, exceeding 800 million dollars. I am currently serving as Chairman of the Board at the Federal Reserve Bank of Chicago, Detroit Branch.

With this background, I have had the opportunity to coach and mentor individuals like Daryll Bryant who are seeking to find their way in corporate America or in the world of mergers and acquisitions. I've worked with Daryll over the last five years and have found his drive, motivation, and experience extremely exciting to watch as he has channeled his experience to achieve his personal objectives. The fact that Daryll has taken the time and effort to frame his experiences in his book *Engage. Lead. Deliver.* says volumes about him as an individual. By expounding on his mentor/employee experiences for the benefit of others who are trying to find their way as leaders, entrepreneurs, and business owners, Daryll is doing exactly what we all should be striving to do: working to support those who will come after us.

Daryll explicitly demonstrates how a good business leader must possess many talents, from the mental fortitude to overcome self-doubt to the ability to talk to people from all walks of life. Transitioning from a college student or standard worker to a business leader presents a unique set of challenges. Throughout his book, Daryll provides wisdom about the fundamental tools which leaders can utilize to make their transition seamless. He relates the experience of his own journey to become an effective leader, including how he overcame the "impostor syndrome" that many leaders face. He also brilliantly outlines a real-life case study from his time as a front-line manager at the M&M Mars company that provides an example of a solution-based team environment.

In recent months, Daryll has expressed a desire to share with future leaders his experiences of leading others within Fortune 100 corporate environments for the past 25 years. His intention is for New Leaders to accelerate their career growth and establish confidence in their leadership abilities. Daryll Bryant's book *Engage. Lead. Deliver.* is a must-read for New Leaders with less than five years of leadership experience. In this book, New Leaders are provided with confidence that they have what it takes to develop into strong leaders by leveraging their unique gifts. For leaders who are uncertain about their ability to lead others and create the desired business outcomes, *Engage. Lead. Deliver.* provides a support structure of three Leadership Pillars to build upon. I am certain that this book will give unexpected leaders the assurance that they can achieve, lead, and succeed because it provides tools that can be leveraged to lead in today's continually changing business environment. Many New Leaders are recent college graduates who were hired by organizations because they were in the top of their classes and mastered theoretical concepts, but they have yet to master the people dynamics that they will encounter. This book will provide them—and all readers—with a strategy for working hands-on with people to deliver and sustain business results. Leaders who apply the tools and techniques listed within this book will accelerate their growth and ability to take on larger roles of responsibility because their leadership capability will be embedded in a firm foundation of fundamental leadership concepts.

This is an excellent book that is well-organized, engaging, and inspiring. It is a work that can help New Leaders around the world gain confidence in their abilities to lead, inspire others, and let go of the fears that many first-time leaders deal with. Enjoy the journey of leadership, and may you reap the rewards of personal and professional growth by putting into action the concepts that Daryll has so articulately provided you within this book.

**Joseph B. Anderson, Jr.**
Chairman & CEO of TAG Holdings, LLC.
Chairman of the Board, Federal Reserve Bank of Chicago, Detroit Branch

# ACKNOWLEDGEMENTS

In loving memory of Maggie Williams—I will always be in gratitude to you. You gave me my first leadership job as a 5-year-old member of our church usher board. Placing me in positions of leadership at an early age gave me the courage to endure moments of uncertainty. You saw something in me at an early age. Thanks for your love and support. Your impact and presence in my life have been a gift.

To my wife Patricia—you have been my best friend for over 30 years. They say opposites attract. You have been everything that I am not. Your loving spirit has guided me in how to show empathy for others and operate with patience and compassion. When I have been closed-minded, you have been open. When I have been introverted, you have been extroverted. When I have been uncertain, you have been confident. When I have wanted to stop, you motivated me to keep going. Any success I have had in 25 years of working in this industry is your success as well. I could not and would not have wanted to experience any of it without you. The comments of our daughter Kaya as a 5-year-old when you had to travel out of town to care for your grandmother sum up what you mean for our family: "I hope she comes back, because we are nothing without her." You have endured in leading six moves for our family in support of my career growth and always succeeded in creating a comfortable family environment, which allowed us to experience a sense of calm. Thanks for sacrificing your own career opportunities to provide leadership to our family. You have been the caregiver to us all and the cornerstone to our success as a family. Most of all, thanks for believing in me!

To Khari, Kiara and Kaya Bryant—you have been the best children a father could ask for. I am so proud of each of you. Your enthusiasm and ambition for life are magnetic. Thanks for making great decisions and representing yourselves in a positive way. I have always been inspired by your courage when facing change. I know that you have been afraid about the thought of leaving your comfort zone whenever I told you we were moving. I have been impressed with how you always found the confidence to take the first step and make the most of each new opportunity. I can tell you now that I too had fears and apprehension about each change that we journeyed upon. Your willingness to give it a try to support my aspirations gave me courage. Your unconditional love for me gave me the confidence that there was no obstacle I couldn't tackle as long as I could return home to see your smiling faces. Thanks for the laughs, amusement parks, bike rides, family game nights (Risk and Monopoly), movie nights, the experiences of cheering for you at sporting events, and most of all for allowing me to be your dad! The experience of being your father will always be my greatest and most rewarding achievement.

Peggy Boone—Mom, you have always been my example. Your work ethic and desire to see me achieve my ambitions has guided me in caring for my family. The words you shared with me while taking me to school in second grade have been my guiding light and keys to success: "Daryll, get your education, because once you have it, no one can take it from you." Thanks for supporting my desires to go to Tuskegee University to study Mechanical Engineering, even after others told you I would waste your money. I still remember your response: "If he wants to go, I am going to give him the chance, even if he wastes my money." Your belief in me inspired me to succeed, as I knew you were taking a risk on me, and I wasn't going to let you down. I know I will never truly understand the sacrifices you made to support my ambition, but I know my family and I could not have experienced any of our successes without your support and desire to see me succeed. Your guidance and teachings on how to be responsible and what commitment means have formed the foundational principles for my leadership signature. I am forever grateful for all the love you have given me and continue to provide me with.

In Loving Memory of Paul Boone. Paul (Pops), although you have transitioned back to source energy, I would be remiss if I didn't mention what the love you provided to mom and me meant to my development as a man and a leader. Your compassion for family provided our household with love and happiness that many leaders have not been fortunate enough to experience. The term step-father could never fully explain the dynamics of our relationship. Thanks for the memories you created and for supporting my educational endeavors. Thanks for your words of encouragement when I wasn't sure of my direction. Thanks for giving me the confidence to know I would be successful.

Kay Williams—Dad, while I didn't grow up in your household, you were never far away. As I spent time with you, I came to appreciate your fascination with learning, reading, and studying. I was always impressed by your ability to study and master a diverse group of subjects. You taught me that immersing yourself in the endeavor of learning is a fun and rewarding exercise. In my adolescent years, I remember being in your presence and doubting the merit of the ideas and knowledge you were sharing with me. I recall thinking there was no way anyone could know all of that. I can say that as I have experienced learning and higher education from some of the most decorated scholars in the world, I have found all the ideas and concepts you shared with me to be truthful. Many times when these global scholars were introducing their wisdom to me, I recall thinking, "Oh, this must be true because my father taught me that when I was a teenager." Hearing it then for the second or third time, it stuck in my consciousness. Thanks for introducing me to books like *Think and Grow Rich* and the *Laws of Success* as a teenager, which taught me I can attract whatever I want into my life. Thanks for sharing your wisdom. I realize that even when I thought I wasn't listening, I was.

William Jones—Will, we have been friends now for over 33 years. Your wisdom and quick wit have caused me to always enjoy your company. I remember you providing the image of what a leader should look like in 10th grade. While we went to arguably the most dangerous high school in Brooklyn, New York, you would show up each day dressed for success in a different suit and tie, dress shoes, and a full-length wool trench coat. You were dressed better than all of our teachers. In the midst of chaos, you projected the image of an executive. Your courage and willingness to stand out and be an example always remained with me. While I was often driven by the fear of how others perceived me, you were teaching all of us that we shouldn't let our environment define us, but we should instead define our environment. When our school environment wasn't supportive of us striving for higher learning, you and I would go to the school library during lunchtime and share new concepts we learned from subjects of our interests. I am certain your friendship pushed me to succeed and not succumb to the pitfalls of our environment. It has been great to watch your growth as a leader and educator. You are continuing to inspire young people to reach for the stars, including my three children. Watching you give a speech on your passion for a global audience in Croatia has been an inspiration for me to share my passion for leadership and write this book. Thanks for your lifelong friendship and for pushing me to step out of my comfort zone.

Spark Bookhart—We are closing in on 30 years of friendship. As your name suggests, sometimes people need a spark of inspiration to move them in the right direction. I appreciate all of the support you have given me on my journey. You have an uncanny ability to maintain a positive mental outlook no matter how bad things may seem to others. Your ability to see the seed of opportunity in every difficult situation, and your courage to challenge me to step out of my comfort zone, has pushed me to continue growing. I have always been impressed with your ability to see new technological developments and future trends. I remember when you shared with me your insight on a young new bookseller Amazon Books back in 1994 and how you thought they would revolutionize the book retail industry. Your support and friendship helped me grow as a leader. When I didn't want to bring my leadership concerns home for fear of it hurting my family life, you provided an outlet for me to share my challenges. During the times of me existing as a ghost leader, your words of encouragement helped me find my confidence and authenticity. Thanks for your friendship and support.

Juan Williams—You were the first leader to challenge me to step out of my comfort zone and my desire to be a ghost leader. The empathy of your words when you were challenging me taught me what a leader should sound like when they want their direct reports to know they care about them and wish for them to rise to a higher level. I recall you first listing all of the talents you saw that I had prior to telling me that I had the capacity for a lot more. Next, you reminded me I had a responsibility to utilize the gifts that I had been given. Many leaders build habits of pointing out the weaknesses their direct reports need to work on without ever sharing the gifts they see in them. Thanks for holding up a mirror for me to look into and inspiring me to showcase my unique gifts.

Sherman Ayres—I will never forget my first visit to the M&M Mars facility where you were the plant manager. When I first entered the facility, your presence—centered in the middle of the office environment dressed in all white like an Admiral in the Navy—provided a clear mental picture for what leadership excellence looks like. Although the office was filled with 30 or more other people, you projected a leadership presence. They say first impressions mean the most. While I didn't know your role or title when I saw you for the first time, I remember thinking to myself, "Whoever he is, I want to do what he does." When others doubted my capability, you created the opportunity for me to show and prove what I was made of. I remember you telling me, "Alright, when I turn the lights on, you need to come out dancing." At the time you shared those words, I didn't know that you were about to shape my future as a leader. At first, it seemed as though you were only giving me the role as a lowly shift manager—giving me the opportunity to rotate shifts and lead a team of 80 associates while my peers were leading no more than 30. I remember my constant desire to do more or to have a sexy day-shift job. I now understand that by giving me the opportunity to lead a team of 80 associates responsible for the manufacture of a global brand (Snickers Bars), you were instilling supreme trust in my capabilities. That experience provided me with both my bachelor's and master's degrees in leadership. I will always be indebted to you for your willingness to risk your reputation on the abilities you saw in me. As I grew into larger leadership roles, I recognized the foundation to support my success was developed in the trenches of being a Front Line Manager within your M&M Mars plant. The environment of leadership excellence you created, the moral standards for how people should be treated, the expectation of a commitment to safety and quality, and the adherence to the founder's five principles have become the signature for my leadership standard. Thank you for opening the window of leadership to me and helping me see what you saw—my capabilities as a leader.

Bill Porter—I remember the day Sherman Ayres suggested I go and speak to you. He said you need to talk to Bill because "Bill Porter is the smartest man I know." At the time, I had a lot of admiration for Sherman, so his words made me curious to find out why he was giving you such high praise. It only took a short time of conversing with you to understand the truth in his description of you. Your wisdom, combined with your ability to deliver it with humor, enabled me to let my guard down. Releasing my guard was pivotal in me tapping into my authenticity as a leader. I remember the conversation I had with you regarding how to get selected for mentoring. While you shared that most often mentors will select the mentee, I remember thinking, "Well, I am selecting you as my mentor." Early on in my leadership development, you recognized my skill for engaging people and shared with me the value of engagement. I am thankful for your recommendation for me to receive and provide training to other leaders on how to create an engaged team and work environment. When opportunities were presented for me to grow as a leader beyond the current capabilities I had developed, I remembered thinking, "If Bill Porter will answer the phone and share his advice, I am sure I can grow into this role." Thank you for answering whenever I needed you most. While I can write a chapter or two on all the things I appreciate, I believe I can sum it up by thanking you for introducing me to the tools which helped me to recognize my greatest power ... MYSELF!

Victor Crawford—Victor, thanks for opening the door to executive leadership for me. Your support of me taking on the leadership of one of PepsiCo's largest beverage plants was surely met with both angst and doubt. You saw something in me after only a short meeting. When others could quickly recite all of the reasons why I would potentially fail, you created the environment for me to get a fair chance at succeeding. Your support proves that often people only need a fair chance in order to experience success. Thanks for having the courage to take a chance on me. Your willingness to do so has changed my life in a positive way. You gave me the opportunity to walk into the unknown as a leader and really find out what I was made of. The myriad of unexpected problems I experienced in the Pepsi leadership role (Wastewater Treatment Facility) helped me to recognize my abilities to thrive when faced with ambiguity and identify my capabilities to deliver results and transform culture. As a result of this experience, I grew as a leader. I have watched you open similar doors for other leaders to experience who they are. Thank you for operating with courage as you continue to climb the ladder of success. You are an example to all of us leaders who follow in your path.

# INTRODUCTION

How does someone with no prior training and background in professional leadership, armed with only a post-graduate education, succeed in leading people who are far more experienced than they are?

How do new leaders overcome insecurity, anxiety, and fear and gain the respect of people they will be supervising for the first time, some of whom are old enough to be their parents or have been working in this business for longer than the new leader has been alive?

If you are in a leadership position and feel unprepared for your role, this book is for you.

I wrote this book to share my experiences as a first-time leader. It is my hope that in sharing my perspective and my experiences, it may help you as well. This book is for the "unexpected leader" who is promoted into a leadership position for the first time but feels unprepared. It's for you if you find yourself in a position of leadership but are not sure you belong or how you got there. Perhaps you don't know what you should do as a leader or even understand the bigger purpose behind the role.

It doesn't matter if you're an extrovert or an introvert. It doesn't matter if you have a few years of experience or you're the new kid on the block. It doesn't matter if you see yourself as a leader or not. Whether or not you ever wanted to be a leader, here you are ... and you can shine in your new role.

In these pages, you will find the tools and strategies to help you overcome your natural fears and anxiety and get the best out of yourself and your team.

You will learn:

- What to do as a leader (understanding your role)
- How to build chemistry and trust
- How to gain the respect of everyone on your team
- How to get everyone aligned to a common goal

- The secrets of team bonding
- How to build relationships with people
- How not to be intimidated by the role and your responsibilities.

Leadership skills can be developed. By the time you have read this book, you will feel ready to take on the role with confidence!

*"* *COURAGE IS*

*BEING AFRAID*

*BUT*

*JUMPING ANYWAY!* *"*

- DARYLL BRYANT

# SECTION 1:
# THE BEGINNING

The transition from employee to leader is intimidating.

Most first-time leaders, particularly those who have achieved a degree in higher education, find themselves in an entry-level management role where they may have the book knowledge but not the practical on-the-front-lines knowledge. The people they are leading know more about the job than they do. That's enough to make anyone want to close their office door and never come out!

I've had these thoughts racing through my head, and so have many other first-time leaders:

"What if they find out I'm a fraud?"

"What if they find out I don't know anything?"

"What if I screw up?"

"What if they won't listen to me?"

These and other self-defeating thoughts can run wild and lead to severe anxiety and poor choices. In this section, we will explore what people believe about leadership, what leadership really is, and the real challenges new leaders face.

" *DON'T RUN*

*FROM YOUR FEARS:*

*FACE THEM HEAD-ON.*

*LEARN TO BUILD*

*CHEMISTRY AND TRUST,*

*AND YOU WILL SHINE*

*AS A NEW LEADER.* "

\- DARYLL BRYANT

Kayagrams

# Types of leaders

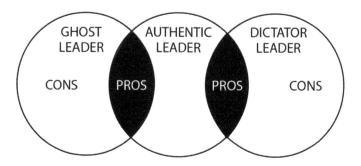

|  | GHOST LEADER | AUTHENTIC LEADER | DICTATOR LEADER |
|---|---|---|---|
| **PROS** | Delegator<br>Approachable<br>Agreeable | Compassionate<br>Approachable<br>Inspirational<br>Collaborative | Decisive<br>Confident<br>Directive |
| **CONS** | Fearful<br>Indecisive<br>Disingenuous | NONE | Iron-Fisted<br>Aggressive<br>Unapproachable |

Kayagrams

# CHAPTER 1:
# THE IMPOSTER SYNDROME

Suddenly, people are calling you "boss." What does that mean?

Does it mean you bark orders all day, and they do your bidding?

Does it mean you're the scapegoat if things go wrong?

Does it mean that nobody will like you anymore, because now you're one of "them" (meaning the stuffed shirts from up high)?

Does it mean you're the one who has to come up with all the answers for every problem?

Thankfully, no. Let's dispel those myths and build a solid foundation on which you can deliver excellence as a leader.

## The Impostor Syndrome

Initially, almost every leader suffers from the Impostor Syndrome. No matter how educated or experienced you are, you feel like a fraud, and you're convinced that everybody is about to find out.

Okay. *Breathe.*

First of all, everybody who has ever come into *any* job feels like a fraud at first (not just leaders). Suddenly, you may be wondering if your resume gave people the wrong impression. What will happen when they find out you feel totally unqualified?

The default mechanism that most leaders will use when they suffer from the Impostor Syndrome is "I'm the boss, and you do what I tell you." Here's a story from my experience that illustrates that impulse.

My first leadership role was at General Electric.

GE had a field engineering program where new engineers were trained to perform maintenance outages on steam turbines and gas turbines that they manufactured and sold to utility companies. The turbines were used at utility power plants to produce electricity. My role was to lead a crew of mechanics, ironworkers, and electricians in performing maintenance outages on these multimillion-dollar assets.

I received my engineering degree as a mechanical engineer. I had gone through about four to six months of training at the GE training center before I walked into my first leadership job out of college. And so I thought, "I'm ready."

My first night at GE, I was supposed to be working with another individual on the night shift.

That night, there was a damaged steam turbine at a power plant. We needed to go in, get the steam turbine repaired, and get it back online so power would be restored to the community.

The expectation was for me to work the night shift alongside an experienced GE field engineer. Prior to my shift, I received a phone call stating that the night shift field engineer would not be in. Something came up, someone was sick at home. He wouldn't be there with me at night, but the experienced field engineer on the day shift would stay later to get me started with the team, and then all I would have to do is monitor things.

When I arrived that evening, the other GE representative from the day shift had to leave early: kid got sick at school, so now suddenly I'm the only one there.

Fresh out of the training center, I come in wearing my bright white GE hard hat ... clean, not a scratch on it ... it was as fresh as I was!

To correct the problem, we needed to maneuver a multi-ton rotor out of a generator housing and attach it to a crane. The crane was positioned outside the building to extend up two stories and boom into the building, attach it to the rotor, lift it up, and take it outside of the wall and down onto a flatbed truck to be transported to the GE center for repairs.

The utility company's plant manager was looking at me like, "Okay, you're going to lead us through this." The hourly workers, millwrights, and electricians were all very seasoned, experienced men, and they all crowded around me and said, "All right, GE, you're the boss! Now tell us what to do."

My heart started pounding out of my chest. Something was telling me, "Okay, you know what to do, just start giving them directions. You've been at the training center." Then there was another opposing force that said, "No, whatever you do, don't do that. *Don't do that.*"

And so, my first decision as a leader was ...

"Let's take a break."

I called a time-out. I backed out of there, and I went down to the parking lot, to my car where I had all my books from the training center. I took a flashlight and combed through the pages of the book to try to find something on this particular issue, reading up on rigging heavy equipment (which we had done at the training center), so I could go upstairs and direct about twenty seasoned men on what to do.

As I'm in the dark flipping through the pages, the thought came to me, "They've been doing this for a long time! Some of them have been doing this longer than you've been alive."

You could say the lightbulb went on in my head.

I said to myself, *"That's it!"*

I went back upstairs after my time-out. I grabbed the group, brought them back together, and said, "Listen men, my goal tonight is to learn from you. I think you know more about how to do this than I do. But if we run into some issues, I have the contacts at GE, I can make the calls and get whatever resources we need to support us."

They all looked at each other then looked at me and said, "This is a smart kid. Get over there, and get you some brats out of the pot, kid. You're going to learn something tonight."

They were sharing their food and inviting me into the fellowship.

*I had been accepted by my crew!*

That was my first leadership moment!

I had to overcome the fear of cranking up my car and just driving onto my comfort zone and giving up, which is the fight-or-flight mechanism that hits you when you're a new leader.

Standing there while they were waiting for me to tell them what to do, I had that initial thought, "Because I have the education, I'm smarter than everybody else. Let me just start telling them what to do."

I'm glad I didn't. I probably would have led us down the wrong path. They probably would have allowed me to go down that wrong path to prove the point, laughing their asses off the whole time.

I'm eternally grateful I didn't give in to that first impulse.

I'm eternally grateful I had the presence of mind to admit, "I don't know what to do."

I earned their respect because I showed them respect and because I showed vulnerability.

When you're new, there are people in the room who know ten times what you know, and you feel like an impostor. They may be older—even your parents' age—and they may see you like a replica of their own sons and daughters. You're faced with the daunting task of overcoming your fears, building respect, understanding everyone's roles, and integrating yourself into the team ... while at the same time keeping the momentum rolling toward the objectives.

The goal is to learn from your people, earn their respect, and build a partnership with them in a way where you can mine their knowledge, skills, passions, abilities, and values. You need to respect them to do that. Your education and experience will definitely come into play, but you want to weave it in and leverage the collective experiences and education of everybody around you.

In hindsight, I wish I could have been a fly on the wall listening to my crew talk about me while I was outside hiding in my car reading the manual!

# CHAPTER 2:
# GHOSTS, DICTATORS, AND LEADERS

The worst part of feeling unprepared for real leadership is coping with fear.

Maybe you're familiar with Star Wars, where Jedi master Yoda says, "Fear is the path to the dark side ... fear leads to anger ... anger leads to hate ... hate leads to suffering."

This quote actually applies perfectly to leadership. Fear is real, and it affects your ability to lead.

You may be leading 5, 10, 20 or more people, and you're the new person. You come into "their" workplace, and you know you're the new kid. You don't know if you'll be accepted or liked. You may feel like you have something to prove. You don't want people to think you don't know anything.

Worst of all, you don't know if you're about to throw a well-intentioned monkey wrench into the works.

What do you do? How do you lead them? How do you support them? When should you step in? How much direction should you give?

At this stage, the initial moment of panic when you realize you're in charge, several types of leaders emerge:

## 1. The Ghost

This type of leader is scared and lets fear take the wheel. And everybody knows it. The Ghost's biggest fears usually revolve around not being liked and about making big mistakes that will make them look bad.

Ghosts hide in their office. Their office becomes their inner sanctum, and the door is rarely open.

They would much rather pull their teeth out than give direction, likely because their own perception of leadership is one where leaders are very dominant. They want to be part of the team but feel totally unworthy of leading. They don't feel strong enough, so they withdraw.

They don't want to take responsibility, so they deflect making decisions, especially the hard ones, so when they're faced with a problem, they let others make decisions (and let the team take the fall if the outcome is bad). They hate telling people what to do, so they let other people run the train, even if the train starts to run off the track. They don't take personal responsibility for decisions.

They despise conflict. They want to be best pals with everybody and not step on any toes, so they prefer not to engage at all and withdraw into the cocoon of their office.

They don't ask for ideas or opinions, and they hate giving honest feedback. Because they're hiding in their office, they have no idea what's really going on, so their decisions are often based on theory but not on real-life situations.

Worse, many of their decisions are based on whether people will like them. Unconsciously, they may sabotage their leadership position.

Because Ghosts are disconnected from the team, they ultimately create an environment of chaos—a free-for-all anarchy that lacks any element of trust and support. As a result, people work without direction or purpose. They don't feel important, and they disengage.

Ghost leaders are weak and ineffective, and the whole organization suffers.

## 2. The Dictator

Dictators lead by terror to mask their own fears and insecurities. Dictators are the classic bullies. You probably know that bullies are extremely insecure, and they bully others just to feel better about themselves.

Dictators are iron-fisted, aggressive, bossy, demanding, usually unrealistic in their expectations, and totally unapproachable. They tell people what to do and how to do it. They micromanage.

They think they know best and never listen to their "underlings." They dismiss people's ideas, which leads to people not saying anything. People fear retribution, so they resort to doing the bare minimum and do their best not to be noticed.

The team will not challenge this type of leader. Instead, they let the leader run into the wall over and over again. The team's productivity drops, and they become disengaged and even subversive, which can lead to an even more iron-fisted approach by this extremely ineffective leadership style. As a result, the whole organization suffers.

\*\*\*

Back to Yoda's quote about fear leading to anger, anger leading to hate, and hate leading to suffering ... even though there may not be outright anger or hate (at least in the case of the "ghost" leaders), *ultimately, both the Ghost and Dictator leadership styles lead to suffering.*

Nobody is happy, nobody feels valued, nobody is productive, nobody feels safe, nobody is proactive, nobody feels heard, nobody cares ... and nothing is accomplished.

In your own experience, if you have had a boss, teacher, or coach who was a Dictator, how did that affect you? Did you feel valued? Were you excited about your work or effort? Did you care? Did you put in extra effort? Did you feel connected to the company's mission and vision?

Have you had experience with Ghost leaders? Did you feel you were making things up as you went along, or did you have clear expectations to live up to? Did you feel you could approach this leader with problems or questions? Did you feel safe? Did you come to work with a positive attitude?

The Ghost and the Dictator are two very separate leadership types, but both are driven by fear. An authentic leader feels the fear as well ... but isn't driven by it.

## 3. Authentic Leaders

Finally, there are the authentic leaders who are willing to move forward to make the best decisions in spite of their fears. Here is a quick overview.

An authentic leader connects people in a way that leverages their expertise, intellect, background, experience, skills, interests, and passions. An authentic leader:

- Values individual contributions and works to bring diverse mindsets together to come up with ideas that are more impactful than ideas from any one individual. As a result, everyone feels they are an important part of the solution.

- Appreciates that many people on the team may be superior in many ways. Instead of being threatened and crushing the "rebellion," the stars are encouraged to contribute.

- Knows that many people on the team may need support in certain areas, but everyone brings something unique to the table and should be encouraged to develop their weak areas and work to their strengths.

- Inspires trust. Everyone knows that the leader will mine them for solutions. They know their opinions count and that it's okay to share ideas even if they are rejected.

- Asks questions and listens more than talks. Even if the answer isn't clear, solutions come from the collective effort and the group-stretch of ideas that comes from facing a problem as a team.

- Accepts negative feedback as a growth opportunity and delivers negative feedback in a way that empowers the individual.

- Gives people the freedom to think and the opportunity to contribute ideas. This encourages them to reach beyond the limits of what they think is possible.

An authentic leader is like an orchestra conductor, bringing individual instruments with unique sounds together to make a beautiful symphony.

At the same time, the leader is "one of us" through common values, concerns, goals, and visions. And the leader is "doing it for us" by looking to advance the interests of the group rather than their own personal agenda.

One of the most heartwarming experiences I've had as a leader was when I received an email from a former team member who had retired after 25 years with the company. He wrote to me, "Thank you for extending my work life and my personal life. You gave me the freedom to do the things that I knew I was capable of."

You can't always choose the people you work with, but you can elevate each team member to reach their full potential. To overcome your fears so you can support each other's weaknesses and amplify each other's strengths, ask the question: "How can I best contribute? What is the best way to showcase my talents, experience, and background to solve this problem?" And then ask the same question as you observe each individual on your team.

# CHAPTER 3:
# BECOMING AN AUTHENTIC LEADER

To become an authentic leader, you need a target to aim for.

What does leadership mean to you? Which leaders do you admire? What type of leader do you aspire to be?

As you're considering the leaders you would like to emulate, it's important for you to know that you really don't have to start off seeing yourself as "leadership material." The truth is, you *are* leadership material, no matter your personality type or background.

Let's dispel some myths about leadership.

# 1. Myth: All you do is give orders.

Perhaps the most common misconception about what it means to be a leader is thinking your job is to tell everyone what to do (and often *how* to do it).

"I'm the boss, so do as I say."

In the last chapter, we talked about the influence of fear. Fear is not something we generally associate with leadership, is it? We don't see the behind-the-scenes battles people fight. We only see the public face, the public behaviors, and we see the results.

# 2. Myth: You need a confident and dominant personality.

Another misconception is that leaders are automatically confident and have dominant personalities. We tend to associate leadership with confidence and dominance, whether those traits are applied by a benevolent leader or by an iron-fisted leader.

Surprise! Confidence and dominance are not necessary leadership traits.

Confidence is certainly useful, but you don't have to be a supremely self-confident person to be a good leader. You can become so good at inspiring your people and overcoming challenges that you will naturally develop confidence over time. And you certainly don't ever have to dominate people to be effective.

However, being overly confident can be seen as being arrogant or dominant and can be detrimental to your role as a leader.

## 3. Myth: You are "above" your followers.

*Leaders are most effective when their behaviors demonstrate that they are "one of us."*

When they are part of the team, not above it. When they want to advance the interests of the group in conjunction with the interests of the organization rather than their own personal interests. When they are able to act in spite of their fears. And when they are able to elevate everyone on the team and motivate them toward a common goal.

Ironically, good leaders are good followers, meaning they are willing to do one thing that domineering leaders are not: they are willing to *listen*. Dominant people don't listen.

# 4. Myth: You have to be a natural leader.

People who perceive themselves as natural leaders are often seen by others as having more leadership *potential* because of the attitudes and behaviors they display, but these people typically don't excel when they're actually in a leadership position *because often they are the supremely self-confident types who don't listen.*

People can fall in love with the idea that people see them as leaders. Being on an imaginary pedestal encourages them to place themselves above and apart from their followers. This destroys their willingness to follow, which translates to mediocrity and ineffective leadership.

Leadership is not about dominating people or forcing them to do something. It's about inspiring them to do something … and beyond that, inspiring them to go the extra mile because they *want* to.

# 5. Myth: You have to have all the answers.

Your job as a leader is to engage people and leverage their experience, intellect, talents, backgrounds, and passions toward a common objective. You're bringing together diverse mindsets with a common goal. You don't have to have all the answers. You just have to empower your team to collectively come up with the answers.

That's when the magic happens. Collective "crowd-sourced" solutions are often more impactful than ideas from any one individual.

Best of all, everyone feels they are a valuable part of the solution and essential to the organization's success.

## 6. Myth: You become a great leader through reading books.

This book won't teach you everything about leadership. It will only give you a foundation. A large portion of your learning will come from your people, the ones on the job, the ones who are intimate with the processes, systems, and problems in ways you can never be.

Although you can't learn all there is to know about being a leader by only reading books, developing yourself by learning and reading will be critical to your success. In Chapter 8, under the section of improvement, I will provide more insight into the role your commitment to reading and learning must play in your leadership development.

\*\*\*

As a young leader, I was most concerned with my own agenda. I was looking to score a project job, which meant working the day shift with weekends off. And I wanted to get my MBA.

I distinctly remember one day when I was sitting in a meeting with the company's HR executive. He asked us what we wanted to do and what our leadership training needs were. I said, "I want to get my MBA." He challenged me by asking, "Why do you want to get an MBA?" I couldn't really give him a clear answer. I just stammered, "Well, an MBA will help me grow in my career." He said that an MBA is good, and it can indeed help you in your career.

But then he said something that was a pivotal moment in my professional life.

He told me that if I would commit to learning how to lead people, *it would do more for my career than getting an MBA.*

That has become a true statement in my experience. I have an MBA from a top-five business school, but I have learned more about leadership by leading teams, making wrong decisions, failing, taking action, evaluating the results of my activities, asking for help, and building relationships with people.

My college and professional education taught me how to think systematically, leverage tools to solve problems, manage competing demands, and develop/execute strategies that support the vision, mission, and goals of the business.

Working with people in leadership positions taught me the power of tapping into the collective genius of the team. Institutional education is valuable, and it will serve its purpose in your growth as a leader, but don't underestimate the power of the ability to inspire and organize a team of people to move in unison toward a common objective. If you will commit yourself to mastering how to tap into your unique gifts and use them to win the hearts and minds (engage) of your team members, you will be amazed by what your team will accomplish and the relationships that will be established.

When you learn how to partner with people that are looking at a problem from many different perspectives, and when you learn to respect everybody's perspective and apply it to the issue at hand, there are no problems that you and your team can't solve. *Nothing.* The power is in the collective.

Learning *how* to lead others prepares you for any role. Wherever your career path takes you, you will benefit from knowing how to inspire, influence, engage, empower and collaborate with people.

*Most of all, leadership becomes less about what your role can do for you and more about what you can do for the role.*

In this section, we discussed what leadership is and what it isn't. Before you read on, please take some time to define exactly the type of leader you envision yourself becoming. That's your target, and the rest of this book will help you hit it!

In the next section, we'll delve deeper into ways new leaders self-sabotage. Knowing what *not* to do is equally as important as knowing what *to* do—might as well save yourself the trouble!

# SECTION 2: THE PROBLEM

You may have heard the cliché that employees don't leave companies, they leave bosses.

In 2015, Gallup surveyed over 7,200 adults and concluded that around half of them had quit a job to escape a manager. But not every employee feels they have the option of leaving, so they stay and check out.

Losing good employees costs an organization a great deal of money, time, productivity, and results. Finding a new employee is one thing. Training them and, most importantly, retaining them depend on good leadership.

I can feel you getting even more anxious now, because you're probably thinking, "Oh great, now there's going to be a mass exodus because of me."

That's not going to happen. Before we get into the specific techniques of becoming a great leader, it's important to look at the mindset of leaders who lose employees and kill productivity.

*"*

*A NEW LEADER*

*MUST OPEN*

*THE PATHWAY FOR PEOPLE*

*TO BRING THEIR*

*UNIQUE GIFTS*

*TO THE TABLE.* *"*

- DARYLL BRYANT

*"*

*WHEN THE*

*GREAT LEADER'S*

*WORK IS DONE*

*THE PEOPLE WILL SAY*

*THEY DID*

*IT THEMSELVES.*

*"*

- LAO TZU

# CHAPTER 4:
# FEAR

We've touched on two types of leaders that emerge from fear. But how exactly does fear drive your behaviors?

After all, no leader would ever admit to being driven by fear, whether they trend toward being a Ghost or a Dictator. However, it's easy to project personal fears into the role … and nobody on your team will tell you that you're a Ghost or a Dictator.

When your professional identity is tied up with your status as a leader, it becomes your only source of self-esteem and self-worth. And that's a very fragile thing.

Here is how fear can affect behaviors:

# 1. Reactivity

Fear stimulates the fight, freeze, or flight reflex. What do fearful leaders do when they're feeling threatened? They lash back at someone who gives them feedback they don't want to hear. They deny a problem and stubbornly carry on. They jump from one project to the next and hope the one with the problem magically resolves itself.

Because they are constantly afraid, they are constantly on the defensive. They are reactive and can't pull themselves out of being hyper-focused on what's going wrong.

# 2. Loss of control

Fear makes some leaders perceive a loss of control of the situation, other people, and/or themselves. In response, they may tighten their grip on others and blow up if their authority is questioned while failing to recognize they can only control one person: themselves.

# 3. Feeling threatened

Fear makes some leaders classify someone as friend or foe, predator or prey. There is no middle ground. The leader feels threatened, even by people who have no interest whatsoever in the leader's position or even recognition. An employee is either with them ("under" or "obeying" them) or they're out to get them. If an employee demonstrates drive, initiative, and confidence, a fearful manager will try to keep that person "in their place."

## 4. Closed-mindedness

Fear makes some leaders blind to other points of view and alternative ideas. At every opportunity, the fearful manager will assert "the way," as in "*this* is how we do things around here" (never mind that the alternative could be more efficient and effective). Fear-based leaders love "sheeple"—people who the leader perceives as empty vessels they can fill with "the way."

Of course, there is no such thing as an empty human vessel. Everyone has beliefs and values; they might not offer to share them, but the ideas are there. If you can coax those ideas out into the light, you may find precisely the right solution to a problem.

## 5. Emphasis on the shiny things

Fear makes some leaders overly focused on extrinsic rewards like higher salaries, professional credentials, performance bonuses, company perks or large departments. They dangle these trophies in front of their employees, just to put themselves a step or two above. At the same time, there is little or no intrinsic reward in the form of satisfaction of a job well done or team spirit.

## 6. Being stuck in the past (in the comfortable)

Fear makes some leaders extremely resistant to change, even if that change would make everyone's lives significantly easier and contribute to greater employee satisfaction and productivity. Fear-based leaders don't want to learn anything new. They already "know it all," so why should they listen to opposing ideas? *The old way has always worked, so why should it suddenly have to be changed and cause upheaval?*

## 7. Addiction to metrics

Fear makes some leaders addicted to metrics. Metrics can become a form of control, but it's fake control. People will often rush through their tasks just to meet some metric, if they feel that it's all the manager cares about, instead of doing their work with excellence because they are motivated and inspired.

One perplexing outcome of this type of attitude is that if someone completes their job efficiently and has time to kill or actively seeks additional responsibilities, the manager becomes upset. Rather than applauding initiative and innovation, they want to see everyone being busy at all times, not be "uppity" and try to outshine everyone else by requesting more work.

Here you have the birth of the term "busywork."

## 8. Lack of transparency

Fear makes some leaders hoard information. They rarely share visions, agendas, values, objectives, or strategies. Somehow, in their minds, this information is on a "need to know" basis that is above their employees' pay grades.

## 9. Lack of boundaries

Everyone's personal time is valuable, regardless of their position. When a leader regularly contacts employees outside of business hours, it's a clear communication that people's personal lives are of no value, and the implied message is that they probably shouldn't expect promotions or even expect to keep their jobs unless they are available 24/7. Lack of respect for people's boundaries and personal lives is fear-based control at its worst.

\*\*\*

All of these traits can be observed in this true example, where the founder/CEO of a small travel company led using fear. This example may shock you, but it is indicative of how fear creates a toxic leader.

After working for several years as a tour guide, Bob opened his own receptive tour company that designed hiking tours for European tourists who wanted to visit the National Parks and sold these pre-packaged tours to big-name tour operators overseas.

For several years, Bob was a solopreneur. He did everything from designing tour itineraries to hiring guides, to booking rooms and excursions, to handling all the administrative tasks, to sales and marketing, to washing out the coffee pot, etc.

As the company became more successful, he hired a small staff. Unfortunately, while he was a wonderful tour guide, he was a terrible boss. Here's why:

Bob was extremely reactive. Any time there was a problem, he would swoop in with accusations and blame. The few times that his employees actually called him out on his own mistakes, he would act like a petulant child and never apologize. Instead, he would turn conversations around and take the focus off himself by pointing out weaknesses in his employees.

Bob micro-managed his employees. He would literally look over their shoulders as they worked and criticize everything.

If something went wrong, he would not have their backs.

Bob competed with his employees. One employee in particular, the Operations Manager, was resourceful and calm under pressure and enjoyed problem-solving. The OM would come up with a better way to handle a recurring challenge, only to be shot down by Bob, who insisted that "the way we have always done it" was better. Most ideas brought up by employees were publicly ridiculed. Eventually, people stopped sharing ideas. Then Bob would complain that nobody showed initiative.

Bob was completely closed off to change, even if it meant greater accuracy and scalability. Where at one time it was possible to run the business with pen and paper, photocopies, staples, and binders, the company had grown. Now it was ridiculously inefficient to not have a computer system to handle repetitive tasks or sensitive issues like hotel reservations and tour bookings. Whenever systems were mentioned, he would snap back, "Well, I was able to do it all this way completely on my own, so why can't you?" … conveniently forgetting that he had run 10 tours per year on his own, and now the business had scaled to 350 tours per year, a number that was being handled by three employees.

Bob constantly changed direction. *Everything* was urgent. He would stop an employee in mid-task and say, "I need you to do this new thing immediately. It's urgent, and it has to get done today." The employee would meekly ask about the current task. Bob would say that it can wait—do this urgent thing NOW. The employee would dutifully complete the urgent task … only to be berated for not finishing the first one! Since everything was urgent, people didn't know what was really a priority, and this led to extreme anxiety as well as rushed work.

Bob could not stand it when people finished what was asked of them and then "get paid to sit around and do nothing." As his employees quietly became more efficient (often implementing their own solutions without telling him, just to make their own jobs easier), they would end up with a bit of free time that eased the pressure of this fast-paced business. Bob completely failed to see that in spite of him, people *wanted* to be more efficient and effective … but when the tasks were done, they would not go to him and ask for more responsibilities. For that matter, they would not go to Bob for anything.

The most telling clue about Bob's fear-based leadership was the extreme turnover in his tiny office. Few employees stayed longer than a year, and many quit within a few months. This meant extreme chaos and inefficiency due to constantly bringing people up to speed as well as an environment of uncertainty, poor morale, and lack of team spirit.

Upon quitting the job after exactly one year, Bob's Operations Manager (the fourth in as many years) remarked to me that although the job caused her incredible stress, it was by far the most enlightening. When I asked why, she said, "Now I know what *not* to do if I ever have my own business. I know how *not* to treat people and how *not* to run a business."

Years later, this former Operations Manager shared with me that she had heard through the grapevine that the business was struggling and on the verge of failing. Is that really any surprise?

Not all leaders are as extremely toxic as Bob of course. Most new leaders genuinely want to be effective as well as have a good rapport with their team. But it pays to be aware of the ways that fear can lead to becoming a toxic, fear-based leader and how powerfully that impacts the business.

# CHAPTER 5:
# THE LEARNING CURVE

Leadership has a learning curve. New leaders rarely fit seamlessly into their new roles, and they will often rationalize and mask their lack of preparedness and leadership skills with behaviors that can undermine their leadership status, alienate their employees, and contribute to a negative work environment.

In this chapter, we will discuss the new leader's learning curve so you can get down to the business of engaging your team.

## 1. New leaders don't always listen.

There is no engagement without listening.

One way new leaders fail is by closing off two-way communication. I struggled with this myself! My first impulse as a new leader was to give direction. I felt that people expected that of me.

I believed that if I was speaking, I was leading.

I believed that if I was telling people what to do, I was leading.

What I didn't realize as a young leader was that *listening is more important than speaking.*

There's a constant battle with listening and speaking, and that's why I make the point that when coming into a new leadership role, you already bring some intangible tools or strengths you can leverage. You could be quiet and good at listening, which is helpful in soaking up information. You can be good at speaking, which would make you charismatic, inspirational, and motivational. But it's as though those two opposites are always in competition with each other. It's not until you recognize the importance of listening and getting people's ideas that you can really capture it.

There was a night I was responsible for manufacturing Snickers, a brand that families love. Our facility made most of the Snickers for the United States. In my training, we were taught that the number one goal is to deliver quality, protect the brand, and ensure that we do everything in our power to not have any recalls or delays to the market because of internal mistakes.

On this night, I was taking over for the previous shift manager. I was a frontline supervisor, but at night I was also the plant manager. I was the head of quality and safety. This responsibility fell to me, because all the other leaders would go home in the evening, and I would be there throughout the night.

That night, the metal detectors alerted, saying that we potentially had metal in the Snickers bars. There's a big risk there as a plant manager. Do you just assume the metal detectors aren't working properly, or do you assume there is really metal finding its way into the candy bars? While I was a frontline supervisor, I was also a father with three small children who adored the products we made. For me, the choice was clear: protect our consumers!

Shutting a line down for hours while you do diagnostics can have serious ramifications, not only in production but also in the marketplace. We were making a product for 60 to 70 percent of the entire country, so any gap in production would show up really quickly in the marketplace. Every hour of downtime for the production process cost the company several thousands of dollars.

As the manager, I stopped the line and brought the department leaders of my team into the conference room. We talked about what we knew, and then I opened the floor with the question, "What do you think?"

That was a key moment in solving this issue. I had my preconceived notions, but something special happened when I opened up the floor, because it created a dialogue between each department.

There was immediate input from the leaders within the interdependent teams from the different departments, and we were quickly able to come up with a list of diagnostic checks to pinpoint where the issue was. I brought together leaders of the quality team, maintenance team, candy processing team, and the packaging team, and we all brainstormed ways to identify the potential issues. To minimize production waste, we developed plans to cycle the process intermittently to help us understand if our actions eliminated the risk of metal contamination.

Everybody left with a game plan to go back to their stations, work with the rest of their teams to run diagnostics, and use problem-solving tools to find the root cause (we used ISO checklists, Fishbone Diagrams, and 5 Whys documents).

We agreed to come back hourly to share our findings and figure out how to go forward. We probably did this for about 6-8 hours during the night. We would start up the process, run for a little bit, get information, bring the information back to the group, share what we learned, discuss options, and come up with next steps. By contrast, if I was acting like a Dictator leader just giving orders to everyone on what to do and how to do it, I would have restricted the flow of the group's ideas toward the problem and turned them into robots, waiting for the next command. Working in a manufacturing environment of approximately 1000 people, where the metal issues could have had a multitude of potential causes, a dictatorial leadership approach would have extended the issue to last two to three times longer. Had I given the team the wrong direction, and they acted on it without sharing their concerns, I may have caused a product recall or been terminated.

Instead of giving orders, I encouraged my team to contribute and collaborate. My team of associates had been working in the facility for 10, 15, 20 years. Not only did they have a depth of experience I would never possess, but they were also intimately familiar with the procedures, processes, and quality checks. Since they spent 10-12 hours per day performing the required daily job tasks, they were the experts whose opinions I relied on. My role was to ensure that we stayed grounded in the organization's values (the consumer is our boss, quality is everybody's job), we followed our quality systems and procedures regarding metal contamination, and we utilized the pertinent problem-solving tools to find the root cause.

While the teams were running diagnostics, I was on the phone trying to contact my superiors, but since it was the middle of the night, I wasn't able to get the right people on the phone. I trusted the process, the dialogue, and engagement with the people on the plant floor. Together, we worked through the problem.

We found the issue and solved the problem without allowing any product with metal contamination to leave the plant. We didn't create interruptions within the marketplace, and we minimized production waste, since some "test Snickers" had to be sacrificed in the testing process. In the end, we all took pride in the fact that our efforts ensured we didn't put the health and safety of our consumers at risk.

As a leader, there's no way I could've done all of that on my own. If I had tried to think of ways to diagnose the problem on my own ... if I had tried to walk everybody through the diagnostics and solutions, there's no way I would've uncovered every possible glitch in the system or come up with the solution as quickly and efficiently as the team could working together. Leaders should spend a large portion of their time ensuring they have the proper talent on their team. When issues arise, allow team members to apply their talents by asking questions that will foster their contribution, like "What do you think?"

The next day when the facility leaders came in, I was able to walk them through point by point: what we did, why we did it, and what we found. I explained that we didn't produce much product tonight, but we found the problem and solved it, no product left the plant, and we didn't generate a lot of waste.

As a result, we received a lot of praise for the methodical way we worked through the process.

I learned at that moment the power of a collective group of people working together with the focus of a common goal. My role as a leader became a lot clearer that night. I realized that it's not that I'm the smartest man in the room, it's not that I'm the engineer … it's that I set the pathway for people to bring their unique gifts to the table and collectively work toward a solution.

Just because you're the boss, doesn't mean you have all the answers or that you are always right.

Without the ability to listen, you are closed off to employees' ideas and solutions. Without open communication where people's ideas are valued, nobody will step up and tell you that you're wrong. They will just let you keep digging … and digging … and digging.

It's not easy to give negative feedback, and it's not easy to receive it. But there can be no improvement unless you're willing to listen to people when they want to tell you what's not working. People need to feel they can talk openly with leaders with no fear of retribution, whether or not there is agreement. Strong leaders encourage feedback, while weak ones avoid it or respond negatively to it.

## 2. New leaders may not invite engagement.

If you don't invite engagement, it won't happen.

You might be the nicest person in the world. You might desperately want to be a good leader. You might genuinely respect employees. You may say you have an open-door policy, but your behaviors may betray you.

Instead of projecting trust and making people feel safe if they need to share some bad news, you may unconsciously give off an insecure "I can't handle that" vibe. And guess what? Nobody will step forward to keep you abreast of what's really going on.

Most communication is nonverbal, so you've got to *show* people, not just *tell* them, that you are approachable. This can be tough if you're a shy or introverted leader, but you only have to suffer through the initial discomfort. Once you get to know your team and establish a rapport with them, you will relax, *they* will relax, and you will both find it easier to engage.

However, the initial invitation has to come from you!

## 3. New leaders may not inspire trust.

Without trust, there is no movement toward goals.

Lack of trust is a tremendous barrier to success as a leader. You have to trust your team to do the work, but your team has to trust you too. They need to know you value them, you have everyone's best interests at heart, you have their backs, and they are safe working for you.

Lack of trust directly affects productivity. Productivity tanks if a team feels a lack of trust. Trust erodes due to lack of communication about where the organization is going, why, and what everyone's role is in making it happen. It also occurs when a leader changes direction often, calls everything "urgent," and withholds information. Nothing gets done when people are sputtering around and not really moving the organization in the direction of its goals.

This stagnation affects everyone. Employees don't have clear direction; the leader is in a mad scramble to get things done; everybody is reactive and feeling like they're constantly putting out fires; and there is lack of respectful interaction or sharing of ideas. Chaos is a severe career-limiting move for leaders!

Inspire trust by coming to them and asking for their input. I did that in the Snickers story. I decided I would no longer tell them point by point what to do. I would give them a set of goals and *let them tell me the best way* to reach those goals. Once they saw I was serious, that inspired the trust. The moment you ask, "What do you think?" you engage them and they trust you, because they see you're serious about wanting their input.

\*\*\*

The Snickers story wouldn't have happened the way it did if I didn't listen, if I didn't inspire engagement with the team, and if I didn't inspire trust.

The takeaway from this chapter is this: walk around! Have some dialogue with people before problems ever arise, just to let them know you're a regular person. Learn more about them. Let them know you value them, because you're willing to ask about things they enjoy outside of work. And when things go south, ask for their input, not as subordinates but as equals.

*"*  *RESULTS*

*BEGIN AND END*

*WITH LEADERSHIP.*

*LEADERSHIP*

*SETS THE TONE.* *"*

\- UNKNOWN

# CHAPTER 6:
# LEADERSHIP FAILS

Even leaders of very successful organizations have been
known to make questionable leadership decisions. The
following examples generally refer to lack of engagement
between top leaders (CEOs, etc.) and their employees.
Within each example, think of how differently the situation
could have turned out had there been open communication
and engagement.

## 1. Tony Hsieh – Zappos

Tony Hsieh, CEO of online retail giant Zappos, decided to
create a new workplace model that eliminated all bosses in
favor of self-management. This model, called holacracy, was

intended to help create a state of organizational enlightenment called "Teal."

The Teal paradigm is a management philosophy characterized by decentralized self-governance and self-selected and fluid roles where people's actions are guided by the organization's purpose and not by orders from leaders. People are encouraged to bring "themselves" to work instead of checking themselves at the door and coming to work as a narrowly focused "professional" self.

The organization is seen as a living thing. Instead of setting goals for the organization, the organization's members are encouraged to listen and understand what the organization wants to become and what purpose the organization wants to serve.

(I swear, I am not making this up. Google "Teal Organizations.")

The result at Zappos was a tidal wave of exits. 29% of the Zappos staff turned over within a single year. The company is still recovering.

Hsieh, it could be argued, did employ the principles of engagement leadership at Zappos, but perhaps the key here is that it was a lack of *leadership* that caused havoc.

People do need a sense of direction. They need to know what to expect. They need to feel that they are safe. It's difficult to achieve those basic objectives in a free-for-all corporate culture.

## 2. Steve Ells and Montgomery Moran – Chipotle

For many years, the burrito chain Chipotle was lauded for its high-quality fast food. Recently, the company has been plagued with numerous serious foodborne illness outbreaks that include E. coli, salmonella, and Norovirus.

Co-CEOs Steve Ells and Montgomery Moran give us the perfect example of what not to do in a crisis. Instead of taking responsibility, finding the source of the contaminants, and working with their employees to correct the situation and regain customer trust and market share, they did what appeared to some to be finger-pointing.

First, they challenged the Centers for Disease Control and the media for sensationalizing the company's problems. Ells then said on national television that Chipotle was the safest place to eat now that the company had implemented new food safety measures. This turned out to be a false statement, as more Norovirus incidents occurred *after* these measures were taken.

The result: the company is facing a federal investigation over food safety issues. Sales have plummeted, putting thousands of jobs at risk.

Things could have been different had the CEOs inspired their employees to communicate workplace hazards. I cannot believe "nobody" knew what was going on given the multiple breaches of food safety. Yet, given the response of the CEOs, it's possible to infer that if Chipotle employees knew that corners were being cut or safety protocols weren't being followed, why did they not communicate that? Did they not feel safe in providing that feedback? Or, if they did communicate their concerns, were they not heard?

## 3. Kay Whitmore – Kodak

One of the biggest mistakes a leader can make is failure to adapt. Kodak, based in Rochester, NY, was once an iconic name in photography. The company dominated the consumer photo market until the mid-1980s when Fuji began offering similar film for less than what Kodak was charging.

1990s-era CEO, Kay Whitmore, made two devastating assumptions that sent the company into a tailspin:

1. The Kodak brand name would win over price competition from Fuji (wrong)

2. The fledgling digital photography industry would never take off (also wrong)

Even though Kodak scientists invented the first digital and first megapixel cameras, the company did not commit to digital photography. We all know what happened next. The demise of film was astonishingly fast and even the giant, Kodak, toppled.

Today, Kodak is trying to rebrand itself as a digital imaging company with mixed results.

What might have happened had Kay Whitmore listened to the company's scientists and asked them what *they* thought of the future of digital photography?

# 4. David Kearns – Xerox

A similar fiasco occurred at Xerox. Xerox was once "the" name in photocopiers (weren't they always called "Xerox machines"?).

It was actually Xerox scientists who invented desktop computing (PCs) and Ethernet. And yet Xerox leaders made fateful decisions including ordering Xerox engineers to share their technology with Apple technicians and Microsoft. With the help of the innovations from Xerox engineers, Apple and Microsoft dominated personal computing in the 1980s, while Xerox's presence as a leading-edge tech company virtually disappeared.

According to a former Xerox scientist (one of the inventors of the photocopier), "Kearns was an idiot bean counter who didn't know what he had, because he couldn't understand what the scientists were talking about."

It's unrealistic to expect a leader to know everything, especially in the fast-moving technology space; however, the Xerox scientists knew they were on to something *BIG*. They communicated the potential of what they had discovered, but their vision was dismissed by their bosses. There was clearly a disconnect between the upper management's vision for the company and the engineering/research team's vision.

What might have been different had the CEO and board of directors *of a technology company* actually listened to ideas from the people developing the technology? What might have been different if upper management shared the vision for the company and not dumped millions into developing technology it didn't even see as a viable step forward?

## Side Note: Steve Jobs – Apple

Clearly, Apple is not a failure. It remains the most widely known name in PCs and personal technology. I'm sharing this example to illustrate just how complex leadership is and that it's possible to have a leader who is deeply engaged and passionate yet still a heavy-handed Dictator who doesn't display compassion.

Steve Jobs was an iconic leader but not always for the right reasons. While his brilliant mind was focused on innovation, he was famous for pushing his employees to the breaking point.

According to a former Apple employee, people would avoid getting into the elevator with Jobs lest he ask them the dreaded question, "So what do you do at Apple?" If they would blurt out their job description, Jobs would snap back with "Yeah, so what do you actually *do?*" Jobs was famous for reducing people to tears and making them sacrifice everything to meet deadlines.

In the case of Steve Jobs, however—even though I've listed him in the "leadership fails" category—the picture is more complex.

It is well known that Jobs could be arrogant, dictatorial, and often just plain mean. And yet he was instrumental in creating the cult-like following that Apple still enjoys. It could be argued that his leadership style was situational and that if he were a gentler, kinder leader, Apple would not have achieved the same spectacular results.

Despite his infamous temper, Jobs did have several leadership qualities that mattered: first, a clear vision for the company that was nothing short of thrilling for Apple employees, and second, an ability to inspire trust because of his genius in product design and marketing as well as his unwavering passion and commitment to the company and its people.

Jobs listened deeply to his employees (although he would famously explode if he heard something he didn't like). He respected ideas and disrespected people who didn't share ideas. He inspired people with his vision, which motivated them to push their own limits of what they thought was possible ... yet at the same time, he would bully them into basically living at the lab until a deadline was met.

The main point I want you to take away from the failures of top Executive Leaders of major corporations is that failure is inevitable. You will make mistakes, and you will experience failures many times throughout your leadership journey and career. The only way to never experience failure is to do nothing, but doing nothing will not support growth. Don't try to be perfect. Take actions, learn from your actions, and ask questions to gain understanding. Although your goal will be to operate as an Authentic Leader, at times you may find yourself trending more toward the Dictator or the Ghost. It's okay. When you recognize where you are, steer yourself back to where you want to be. Don't let fear's first cousin, guilt, sink in. Self-reflect, forgive yourself, forgive others, admit when you're wrong, and when necessary, ask for forgiveness. It's all part of the journey of learning.

Oprah Winfrey provided a quote I believe gives failure a proper perspective. She calls it the inevitability of failure: "It doesn't matter how far you might rise. At some point, you are bound to stumble. If you're constantly pushing yourself higher and higher, the law of averages predicts that you will at some point fall. And when you do, I want you to remember this: There is no such thing as failure. Failure is just life trying to move us in another direction." (Harvard Gazette)

In Section 2, you learned how not to lead from some painful examples of how fear can derail even the best-intentioned leader. In the next section, we turn to the positive: how to lead through engagement and compassion.

# SECTION 3:
# THE PAYOFF

I was probably somewhere in my seventh year of leadership when I had an "aha" moment. I had a team of about 80 people, and daily we would attend a team transition meeting from the day shift to the night shift. My team would meet with the previous shift manager who would share with us what happened during their shift. Usually I would sit in the meeting and look around the room to make sure I had all of the people for the critical roles we needed in order to make the transition. I would look around and say, "Joe's here, Mary's here, John's here." But for some reason on this day, when I looked at Joe, my brain said, "20 years of experience."

When I looked at Mary, I thought, "15 years of experience." When I looked at John, I thought, "25 years of experience."

The light went on. I thought to myself, "Wow, they know more about doing this job than I'll probably ever learn. So why am I telling them what to do each day?"

What I did that night—I called it my experiment—is write down all of the key goals that we had to deliver to have a successful night shift. I brought in the leaders from each department, which was 8 leaders for an 80-member team. I shared the goals with them.

I said, "Okay, here are the goals. Whatever happens out there tonight, I want you to make the adjustment to help us reach these goals. Whatever decisions you make, I just want you to explain to me why you made the decision in relation to helping us reach the goal."

I said, "You have any issues? Just give me a call."

That night as I was doing my paperwork, I got a phone call: "Hey, do you want us to increase the line speed?"

I said, "I don't know."

They said, "Well, what do you mean you don't know?"

I replied, "If you increase the line speed, which goals will we reach?"

The voice on the other end of the phone said, "Are you really serious about this?"

I said, "Yep, I want you to make whatever decision you need to make to help us reach the goals."

So they did it. We had one of the best nights ever. The team members would make the decisions and call and say, "We made this decision, and here's how we believe it's going to impact the goal."

Not only did that night go exceptionally well, but in subsequent nights the team leaders would tell me they saw a way to help us stretch the goal. I said, "Tell me more," and they would share ideas about what we could do to move beyond the current goals, and all I needed to do was move the obstacles out of their way. In large part, the obstacles were policies or systems people felt they couldn't challenge. But if I said, "Go for it," that rule went out the window and people were free to tackle the problem with greater efficiency.

That's where I learned if you tap into the collective experiences of people, if you value them, if you show that their opinion counts, something I call magic happens. You deliver results you didn't even dream were possible, and they keep trying to challenge and stretch and do more as if it's their way of telling you thanks for giving them the freedom to think and be leaders as well.

As I grew into larger leadership roles, I continued to go back and reconnect to the lessons of that "aha" moment. I learned that as you grow as a leader, the goal is to be able to take on more responsibility. And you can't take on more responsibility if you believe you have to be in control of everything, if you're the one who has to have all the answers, or if you believe you have to be the one telling everybody else what to do. A leader must develop the skills which will enable them to pull from the collective capabilities of the people on their team. In order to do this successfully, they need to focus each day on assessing and developing the talents and skills their teammates bring to the table.

" *THE DOOR*

*TO UNLIMITED ACHIEVEMENTS*

*WILL OPEN*

*WHEN YOU BEGIN TO SEE*

*THE INNATE GIFTS OF OTHERS*

*AND SEEK*

*WAYS TO SERVE.* "

- DARYLL BRYANT

Kayagrams

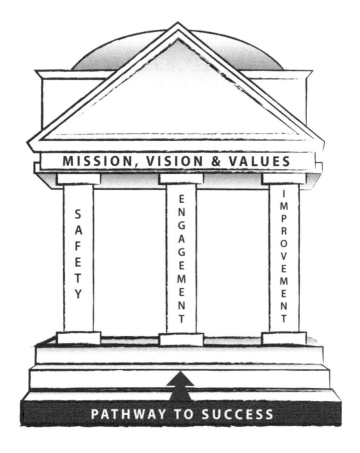

Kayagrams

# CHAPTER 7:
# THE RULES OF ENGAGEMENT

Visualize your role as being supported by three pillars:

- Safety
- Engagement
- Continuous improvement

These pillars collectively support both the organization's mission, vision, and values as well as the needs of every individual within the organization. When you align your actions and choices with these three pillars, you can accomplish extraordinary things.

# Safety

Safety is everything!

Would you go to your boss with a concern or grievance if you thought you would be blamed or fired? No.

Would you feel good about working in an environment hazardous to your physical well-being, knowing that your boss is aware of the situation and doesn't do anything about it? Hell no!

When you don't feel safe physically or emotionally, you will not engage.

In 1997, Paul O'Neill took over as CEO of ALCOA, the world's sixth-largest producer of aluminum. ALCOA was struggling. The Wall Street Journal interviewed O'Neill on how he would make ALCOA competitive again. O'Neill never mentioned numbers. Instead, he talked about taking safety to zero incidents, even though ALCOA's safety record was superior in the industry. As you can imagine, the room went silent. What does safety have to do with the bottom line? O'Neill's point was that if even one person is injured on the job, it's too many, and that if safety is a priority, then productivity, and therefore profits, go up.

Paul O'Neill understood that safety is the foundation for creating engagement. When you ensure a safe work environment, you show your employees you care about them. The cost of safety measures doesn't directly impact the bottom line; it does so indirectly through engagement and productivity. When people get hurt at work, it affects them and their family, but it also has a profound impact on other associates who work within the organization with them. Depending on how bad the accident is, the morale of peers and co-workers may drop significantly. Instead of trying to drive the business forward with new ideas for improvement and growth, associates will be thinking about how they could be at risk for a similar accident.

People didn't believe O'Neill was serious, but he proved them wrong. He gave his employees the power to shut down plants—a shocking move. He made it clear that safety is everybody's responsibility, and everybody should have the chance to correct safety problems. After putting this new practice into place, ALCOA's safety record improved to close to zero if not zero incidents.

It was a full commitment, from the bottom up. The culture at ALCOA became "one for all and all for one." The results?

Greater employee satisfaction, reduced costs, and increased profits.

O'Neill recognized that if people don't feel safe, they will do their jobs but nothing more, and if ALCOA was going to compete, people needed to do more.

I had a real-life experience as a young manager that made Paul O'Neill's viewpoint personal to me.

I was a frontline leader in an M&M Mars candy factory. We were having issues with a conveyor belt jamming and shutting down the line. One night, as I walked through the factory, I noticed two mechanics looking at the conveyor belt the plant had been having problems with.

The maintenance manager and I had been having an ongoing disagreement regarding whose team was responsible for the issues with the belt. We were pointing fingers at each other, but the root cause of the problem was not being solved. As I approached the mechanics, I asked them if the conveyor belt was having an issue and they said, "No, we're just monitoring it to see if the issue occurs again."

I left them to go speak to my colleague Eddie. As I approached Eddie, he turned around in a dead sprint and ran in the opposite direction. I grew up in New York City, and when I see somebody take off running with no explanation, I know it's probably a good idea to take off running too, so I went into a dead sprint after him. I didn't know why we were running, but I figured whatever it was, it was behind me. We probably ran for about 40 yards down to the end of the factory. When I caught up to him, I said, "Hey, why are we running? Is something wrong? What's going on?"

Eddie said, "Yeah, the candy crashed on the end of the belt. I was coming to try to keep it from making a big mess."

I was thinking, "Okay. I thought somebody was injured or something."

As I was trying to help Eddie clear the jam, another person came up to me and said, "Daryll, I think somebody's hurt at the other end."

I said, "No, you're mistaken. I just came from there and nobody's hurt."

He said, "No, Joe just got his arm caught in the machine."

I'm thinking, "Fuck, I just left from up there."

I ran back to see that Joe's arm had slipped in between two conveyor belts. The belts pulled his arm in almost all the way up to his elbow before someone was able to pull the emergency stop. The mechanic helping Joe was almost in a panic trying to disengage the rollers to remove Joe's arm.

In my mind, it looked like the machine was eating him alive. It was really gruesome to see! And the only words Joe could manage when I came up to him were "Don't cut the belt."

I was almost in a state of shock, but then his words snapped me out of it. I said, "What did you say?"

Joe didn't want to destroy the company's equipment to get his arm out of the machine! He was so committed to his job! He cared more about the company than he did his own arm.

I pointed at one of the other mechanics and said, "Cut the belt! Destroy whatever you have to, just get his arm out of that machine!"

We were able to get his arm out and took him to the hospital. He ended up with nerve damage, but his arm was saved.

I learned a powerful lesson that day. Leaders: *your people are listening to everything you say.* Joe was so committed to my daily discussions regarding improving productivity that he was worried about destroying the company's equipment more than the condition of his arm. That day, Joe and everybody else learned that I valued *them* over profits.

I didn't realize it at the time, but later it became clear to me that I failed as a leader that day! Instead of pointing fingers and debating with the maintenance manager about whether his team or mine was responsible for the repeated failures with the belt tracking off its path, I should have partnered my Production team with the Maintenance team to determine the root cause for the failures. If my leadership had engaged the associates to use continuous improvement tools to resolve the repeat issue, the maintenance mechanics would not have needed to be monitoring the belt, and Joe probably would not have moved his hand onto the rollers. Once I walked up to Joe and learned that he was monitoring the belt, I should have reaffirmed, "Hey, Joe, you're not putting your arm near the belt to clear a jam, right? If you have to clear a jam, be sure to shut the machine down and lock it out. It's okay for us to have the downtime in production if you need to work on the belt, because I want you to work safely."

Sometimes it's just a little reminder. I didn't know Joe was going to stick his arm in there, but I could have reaffirmed to him that stopping the line to correct an issue and ensuring all safety protocols were adhered to was more important than keeping production going, and it had to happen regardless of cost.

*Safety first.* It doesn't matter whether you're in a manufacturing plant or whether you're in sales. You need to ensure that:

- People are conscious about the risks in the work that they do.
- People can raise concerns about potential risks.
- People have the resources to put solutions in place to mitigate those risks.

I was sharing insights on a leader's role in ensuring a safe working environment with my 18-year-old daughter Kiara. She said, "I get that. If the company doesn't care about me, why should I care about it?"

As an employee, doesn't it feel great to know that your boss cares enough about you to make sure you're safe, comfortable, and happy?

I was in a Chick-fil-A restaurant one evening. I had finished my meal and was walking out the door. I overheard a manager tell one of her employees whose shift had finished, "Have a safe drive home." I noticed this employee was pregnant. The manager added, "And be sure you watch out for deer while you're driving."

It's so easy! Just show people that you are concerned for their well-being with a simple reminder like, "Watch out for deer" or, "Make sure you don't text while driving."

## Engagement

One key element of engagement is compassion. Unfortunately, compassion is not something often talked about in business circles. Compassion simply means that you care. You desire to make someone's life better through respect, listening, empathy, concern, and support.

Compassion is listening with empathy to people's concerns, ideas, and opinions; making them feel important; making them part of the solution; encouraging them to utilize their unique talents, experience, skills, and passions in their role; and uplifting them to be the best they can be.

At Pepsi, where I was now in the Plant Manager role, we had an issue where bottles would fall over after exiting the filling machine. The filling machine operator would stand up each bottle after it had fallen over. This was clearly not a great use of a human resource, so I asked him how often the problem occurred. He stated that he spent most of his shift (10 hours) walking around the machine to stand up bottles to ensure they didn't cause further downtime issues to equipment downstream of his machine. When I asked him why he didn't raise the issue to his managers to have the problem corrected, he told me he did. He was told that they were not going to fix the issue for him because his machine was not a priority within the plant. He was told he needed to live with the issue because, as a machine operator, he was being paid to stand up every bottle that falls over.

I said to this associate, "We'll have this fixed for you by morning."

I want to emphasize that I said "for you," because it really was not just for the company's benefit but for this associate's benefit as well. His job would feel more meaningful if we showed we cared about him.

I explained to the managers that if we wanted to leverage the collective power of our people, we had to take care of the low-hanging fruit issues that come up. I challenged the managers to do everything within their power to create a long-term fix overnight so the bottles wouldn't be falling over by morning. During our dialogue, I asked them to think about whether we would get more value out of our associates who operate machine centers by having them perform routine repetitive tasks which we could repair, or by asking them to monitor the processes within their machine centers and share opportunities for continuous improvement with leadership.

I didn't tell them how to fix it. I wanted them to take the lead and solve the problem in the way they felt was best.

The next morning, the first thing I did was walk over to the machine that had been causing the bottles to fall over. In the place of one old wooden leg was a metal leg. I said to the operator, "I see the wooden leg is gone. Did that help?" He put a big smile on his face. He said, "Oh my gosh! It's running so much better already within the first hour—I haven't had any bottles fall over!" My team solved the problem by leveling the machine and adding a sturdier metal leg, which minimized the vibration causing bottles to topple.

The problem would not have been solved as quickly and ingeniously if I had given a directive! I wanted to ensure we were creating a culture of continuous improvement. You're *not* doing that if associates are sharing issues that are negatively impacting the operations and instead of partnering with them to identify possible solutions, you tell them, "It is not a priority; continue to run around the machine and stand bottles up. That's your job." Why would anyone ever share their ideas for improvements with you? Developing an environment of continuous improvement within your team will help to minimize chaos and operational crisis situations. However, issues will arise and a crisis will come up. It happened to me on my first night at GE: I walked into a crisis. When you ensure the low-hanging fruit issues are resolved within your team (the issues that make their jobs harder to perform) and they have the tools they need to perform their jobs, they will show up to crisis situations fully engaged and eager to support you.

## Improvement

At Diageo, where I was in a Vice President of Manufacturing role, we wanted to introduce a new product to the market, but our manufacturing equipment wasn't able to produce a quality product. Whenever we ran the product on the line, bottles would get splattered with sticky sugary liquid. We couldn't send it into the marketplace like that, but corporate leaders, marketing executives, and sales executives said this product was critical to the company's goals.

We were the only manufacturing option available ... so how were we going to fix the problem? At first, it seemed like a lost cause. We *could* have said that we can't run this product because our current process isn't capable of running it ... and hire people whose only job was to clean the bottles. That solution was not feasible anyway since we were running 800-1000 bottles a minute!

I saw the issue from both sides, and I challenged the team by asking what's possible. I said, "What can we do now, and what can we do long-term? It's definitely not feasible to just wash the bottles, but I will support us doing that in the short term."

We needed a robust, long-term solution. I gave them the "why" behind it. I explained to them what was going on in the marketplace. I explained to them why this product was critical to the business, and I explained to them what was in it for them as well if we were successful and hit our key business goals.

As a result of that dialogue, the team came up with a new solution. They installed what I called an in-line car wash with air hoses and water jets on the conveyors. As the bottles came down the line, water jets would spray them clean, and then air knives would dry them so labels could be applied.

The team's ingenuity brought the in-line car wash idea to fruition. They came up with a path forward, because they understood the goal and the challenges, and they knew I trusted them to find a solution.

We met the goal. We were able to manufacture all of the product we needed and distribute a quality product that proudly represented the company's standards and inspired customers to purchase it.

Improvement never stops—and the best ideas for improvement often come from the people on the front lines!

# CHAPTER 8:
# PRACTICAL TIPS FOR
# ENGAGEMENT

Now you know the fundamentals for what it takes to be a great leader (safety, engagement, and continuous improvement), and it's time to put it into practice.

## Safety

Your fundamental responsibility as a leader is to ensure the safety of your employees. It may seem obvious in an industrial setting where there is the very real danger of physical harm, but even in low-risk environments like an office, where you might think the greatest hazard may be getting a paper cut, employees could be exposed to potential safety issues, including:

- Faulty wiring
- Lack of electrical outlets, requiring the use of extension cords
- Risk of slipping/tripping/falling
- Blocked emergency egress due to lack of storage space
- Inadequate or harsh lighting, leading to eye strain and fatigue
- Poor ventilation
- Awkward furniture or equipment layouts that invite collisions or accidents
- Misuse of equipment, such as using a rolling desk chair as a step stool
- Accidents and injuries due to stacking and lifting
- Ergonomic factors including chairs and keyboards
- Noise pollution
- Improperly marked or unmarked exits
- Lack of GFCI outlets in the breakroom or near a coffee machine
- Environmental toxins ("sick building syndrome")
- Lack of an emergency response plan

When you look around—really look at the environment your employees are working in—think about safety this way: if people don't feel safe, they will waste time and energy trying to become safe. If safety issues are taken care of, they can focus on their jobs. You always have the potential to improve your team's work environment, and doing so demonstrates that you care. When you care, so does your team. Try the following ideas to ensure the safety of your employees:

- Tell your traveling sales representatives to put the phone down while driving.
- Hold fire drills.
- Make sure that your desk-bound employees have ergonomic chairs and keyboards.
- Improve task lighting.
- Create a comfortable and quiet work environment.
- Pay attention to space layout to make sure it's easy and safe to move about, and that all exits are clear and clearly marked.
- Make sure people know what to do in an emergency.
- Listen when someone alerts you to a safety issue, even if it's just a request to move a file cabinet six inches because it's hard to maneuver the mail cart around it without bumping into the water cooler.

- Make sure the building's electrical and plumbing systems are up to code.
- Show people where the emergency exits and fire extinguishers are and how to use fire extinguishers.
- Distribute a contact list of employees and have an emergency response plan that includes a check-in procedure in case of evacuation.

Above all, listen to what people actually need and see their role from their perspective. There will always be things they have to deal with on a daily basis but for whatever reason don't communicate. Just by bringing them together and having a conversation about what they actually need, you create more productivity.

## Engagement

Engaging your team is your superpower as a leader. Even if you're shy, even if you feel totally unprepared for the role, there are things you can do to create an instant rapport with your team.

Even if you don't see yourself as a leader, others do—and if not immediately, then they see your potential—which is why you're here in the first place. The person who promoted you to that position obviously sees leadership in you.

But *how* do you walk into this foreign environment where you feel like an outsider? How do you actually harness your inner traits?

What is the first thing you can do to ensure you're not going to be a complete screw-up? What's the first thing that you can do when you walk in there on day one, feeling totally unprepared and freaked out, when you're ready to just curl up in a ball and crawl back under a rock?

Theory is nice, but let's get down to the practical ways to build your leadership skills.

## 1. Get to know people.

The first thing you do as a new leader is to get to know people. Introduce yourself. Greet people with a smile. Let them know who you are, and get to know them. Spend as much time talking about them as they're comfortable. *Show genuine interest in the individuals on your team.*

Believe it or not, this initial step is great news for the introverted or shy leader. Why? Because after the initial awkwardness, when you settle into being genuinely interested in people and asking questions about them, you put the focus on them and take it off yourself. After that, you've already established a connection and it's much easier to talk to them.

## 2. Be approachable.

Be available and approachable when people need you, not just when it's convenient, so those small problems can be addressed before they become huge. Always take the attitude of being there to support your team rather than making them feel that you're being inconvenienced with questions or concerns. Make them feel *safe* sharing concerns, problems, and ideas.

## 3. Focus on development

One of the best ways to unite a team is to give them a common goal, but in any group, there are poor performers. Instead of targeting them, focus on developing those people. This sends a powerful message: we're all in this together. We're a team. We build each other up, and we don't knock each other down. We find out how to squeeze the best out of everyone, and we do not allow targeting of one teammate. This gives people a sense of safety (again, the "we" approach) which allows them to focus on their role and improve. If given the proper guidance, tools, and support, most people will *want* to do well and make a contribution.

## 4. Lift them up

While all new leaders suffer from the Impostor Syndrome, only weak leaders try to outshine their employees, because they are terrified of working with people who are more skilled, intelligent, experienced, dedicated, or hardworking. If the point of leadership is to get the best out of people, then make them better than you. Develop them. Let them outshine you. Celebrate their awesomeness. Make them feel important.

## 5. Deflect credit for successes and take responsibility for failures

One of the most devastating things you can do as a leader is to take credit for successes and deflect blame when things go wrong. If you want to build engagement and loyalty, deflect credit for successes and give credit to your team. When things go wrong, step up and take responsibility for the failure of your team. This shows your team that you won't throw them under the bus for failures and that you aren't in it for personal glory.

# Improvement

If there's one mantra I encourage you to use whenever you're feeling insecure, it's this:

*Never stop trying to be qualified for the job.*

When you're starting out as a leader, work to your strengths, but never stop improving. Anyone who thinks they've mastered a role will soon be replaced by someone who is willing to hustle, and by hustle I don't just mean work harder, but *innovate, experiment, be willing to fail, and learn.*

The most valuable areas of self-improvement will become apparent if you take the time to periodically do a self-assessment.

It's not easy to do an accurate self-assessment, because we are often blind to our personality traits and behaviors. Discovering that we are not how we see ourselves can be humbling and uncomfortable. However, in the interest of self-improvement, conduct a realistic evaluation of your strengths and weaknesses and how they impact your team.

Self-aware leaders do a better job of engaging a team, because employees do what the leader does, more so than they do what the leader says.

Emotional intelligence is vital for a leader who wishes to lead by engagement. I have a friend who insists, "You can either be intelligent or emotional, but not both," and while I get his point of view (he was talking more about personal relationships than business), emotional intelligence is often perceived as too "soft" for business.

Emotional intelligence is defined as "the capacity to be aware of, control, and express one's emotions, and to handle interpersonal relationships judiciously and empathetically."

Here are some self-assessment questions you may want to visit periodically:

- How do you respond in a crisis: are you reactive or do you respond calmly?
- How do you respond when there is a line at your door of people needing answers *now*?
- Can you manage your emotions in difficult situations?
- Are you comfortable delegating, or do you feel you have to do or oversee everything?

- Do you feel the need to jump in and do it yourself if someone isn't performing a task to your expectations, or do you take the time to work with them or guide them?
- Do you find yourself frequently frustrated at people's lack of initiative or commitment?
- Can you make decisions quickly using the best available information and then, no matter the outcome, take ownership of those decisions?
- Do you understand your team members as individuals with unique skills, experience, traits, knowledge, and passions?
- Do you like to tell people how to do a task, or do you prefer to let them do it their way?
- Do you prefer to have strict control of a situation and people, or do you prefer to receive and consider the input of people around you?
- Do you trust the people you work with?
- Do people feel free to share ideas with you, even if you disagree with their ideas? (Do you value their input? Or if you're not getting feedback and people aren't sharing ideas with you, why do you think that is?)

- Do you prefer rigid rules and structure, or are you flexible and adaptable?
- Do you inspire your team by sharing your vision?
- Are you approachable but at the same time able to maintain your boundaries?
- Do you *show* your team members that you care for and appreciate them?
- What is the way you most commonly show appreciation for your team?
- Do you regularly give constructive and encouraging feedback to your team members and give them an opportunity to improve?
- Do you ever blame people for mistakes?
- Are you transparent in sharing goals, expectations, challenges, successes, and strategies?
- Do you listen and appreciate your team members' input?
- Do you give *and receive* feedback and criticism with grace and dignity?
- Do you give people a sense of safety when they come to you with problems?
- Do you make your employees feel safe at work, both emotionally and physically?

- Do you consider yourself as part of the team, or do you prefer to see yourself as a rung or two above and separate?
- Do you uphold your own and the organization's values?
- Do you demonstrate the behaviors you expect from your team?

Once you've answered these questions, make it a point to improve in the areas that pull you away from being someone who leads by engagement. Periodically take the time to go through these questions again as a way to measure your own growth.

In Chapter 3 Myth #6, I said it's a myth that reading books will make you a great leader. However, reading is essential for your improvement and personal development.

NBA Legend Kobe Bryant explains in a YouTube video titled "Kobe Bryant's Insane Work Ethic" #MentorMeKobe (published March 8, 2018, seen on December 18, 2018) why he started his workouts at 4 a.m. In his video, Kobe states, "If your job is to be the best basketball player that you can, you have to practice and you have to train. You have to train as much as you can as often as you can." Kobe explains that waking at 3 a.m. to begin training at 4 a.m. allowed him to have more training sessions in a day than someone who started later in the day at 10 a.m. He states that committing to this system of training for five years allowed him to be so far ahead of his peers that it didn't matter what type of workouts they tried to do, they could not catch up to him. My challenge is for you to commit yourself to being the best leader you can be. In order to do that, you have to practice, and you have to train. Accepting a leadership role and leading teams of people each day will be your practice. Committing yourself to reading books that will stimulate your mind and applying concepts you read to your leadership practice will be your training.

On your journey to be the best leader you can be, I ask that you attend professional seminars on leadership and personal development and read at least one book per month for the next five years. Like Kobe Bryant, doing this will allow you to separate yourself from your peers. Your growth as a leader will be exponential because at the end of five years you will have read 60 books for your leadership training and development. To help you get started, in Appendix A I have provided you with a list of 60 books from my personal library that have helped me. To make this training seamless, always have a book with you to fill the void of any time spent waiting in lines or sitting on planes, buses, and trains. Download books to your mobile devices. Purchase audio versions of books to listen to while you're stuck in traffic. You have many more options for reading than I did when I started. Find a method that works best for your learning style, and enjoy the process. You will learn so much that your experiences as a leader will be enriched and opportunities for growth will come your way. That's the way it happened for me—the opportunities for growth found me. When they appeared, I was prepared because I had been practicing as a leader and training my mind by reading.

# CHAPTER 9:
# REWARDS OF ENGAGEMENT

Humans are funny creatures. We can be given all the facts, and yet we still make emotional decisions. In this chapter, we will discuss how you will personally benefit and feel after crafting a compassionate and engaging approach to leadership.

The biggest benefit to you from positively engaging your team is that you will succeed in your leadership role, and the role itself is much greater than you. Your role as a leader will allow you to cultivate other leaders and watch them develop their unique leadership signature. You will take pride in knowing they are planting the seeds to grow other compassionate and engaging leaders because you have taught them the fundamentals. Great leaders have an ego, but their ambition is channeled away from personal gain to the greater good.

Success gives you confidence in managing complexity, ambiguity, deadlines, and a wide variety of personalities. That confidence will make you feel like there is no limit to your leadership skills and capacity to deliver outstanding results.

*"Leaders don't create more followers, they create more leaders."* – Tom Peters

After diligently working to develop my leadership skills, I was given my first role as an executive leader by Pepsi. I remember looking at the other plant managers as a frontline leader and saying to myself, "I can do that job. That job is really easy." I would see them sitting at their desks talking on the phone. Easy, right? I remember when my opportunity came—when I was promoted to executive leadership. The first day I walked into my office, it was about 7:00 in the morning. As I closed the door behind me, I saw my big desk, the big conference table, and the big chair. And wouldn't you know it—I pressed my back up against the closed door, and I started taking deep breaths. I felt like I was having a panic attack similar to the panic attack I had my first night at GE when I had to call a time-out to go hide in my car.

I felt myself breathing heavily. I was afraid to go sit in that big chair. That throne, with all the responsibility attached to it. I said to myself, "What should I do?" which was similar to what I said to myself that first night at GE. The thought came to my head, "Do what you do best."

I began breathing deeply, but I felt like I was running out of air and sliding down the door. I thought, "I don't know what I do best."

I thought to myself, "You have to do better than this because you can't have them coming in here and finding you passed out on the floor on your first day as the new executive leader."

I tried to calm myself down. I slowed my breathing and the thought came back to me, "Talk to people."

"I'm a communicator," I reminded myself. "I can talk to people. I'm good at that."

I snapped to attention, now feeling both strong and vibrant, I decided to immediately go out into the manufacturing plant and talk to everyone I came across. *Everyone*. And so I did.

After I finished speaking to every single person I came in contact with, for over three hours, I gained clarity on how to connect with their mindset and what my role and purpose was as their leader.

When I went out and talked to people, my leadership role was no longer about the big desk or the big chair. I didn't have that desk to hide behind, and what I discovered was that *not hiding gave me freedom.*

When I took the time to understand what's going well for the people who work here and what's not going well, I built a rapport. That rapport gave me the wings to take the organization—and all the people involved in it—to new heights.

There's really no problem that's unsolvable when you go out and talk to people and tap into their collective genius.

*"A leader is best when people barely know he exists, when his work is done, his aim fulfilled, they will say: we did it ourselves."* – Lao Tzu

The challenges you will face will be similar, no matter the industry. You'll ask yourself (probably in a panicky state): "What do I do now?!"

The answer is do what you do best. What's that? What do you do best? Be authentic! Here are nine leadership tenets that will help you, right now, as a new leader and years down the road when you're at the top of your game:

1. Go out and talk to people.
2. Learn about yourself. Leverage your unique gifts to develop your leadership signature.
3. Take care of your people (and they will take care of you).
4. Bridge the needs of the people with the goals of the organization. Share the vision and let them share ideas for how to achieve it.
5. Focus on quality and excellence in everything you say and do. Lead by example.
6. Empower people: ensure their opinions count and engage them in the idea process.
7. Listen. Everybody needs to be heard.
8. Don't run from your fears: face them head-on.
9. Channel your ego away from yourself and into the larger goal, building a great team and a great company.

And now, you have the keys to become successful in any leadership role!

I will emphasize again: you can become a great leader, even if you feel unprepared right now.

Throughout this book, I have been giving you the fundamentals to great leadership. I hope you can see it's not difficult. There will always be more to learn on your road as a leader. After 25 years, I am still learning. What I have shared with you are the building blocks which should form your foundation. You *can* do this, even if you feel unprepared!

The number one thing you should take away from this book is this: effective leadership relies on the ability to engage your followers. The key to success is thinking in terms of "we," not "I."

- You have learned how not to lead (as a Ghost or a Dictator).
- You are now familiar with the ways that fear can derail your best intentions.
- You have seen powerful examples of what works.
- You have learned how to identify the traits you already possess that you can leverage as an emerging leader.

- You have learned the simple steps to begin leading your team by establishing a foundation for safety, engagement and continuous improvement.

These simple techniques are the easiest and most effective way to leverage the strengths of your team, increase productivity, and successfully achieve a common goal.

You don't have to perceive yourself as a natural leader. *Leadership is a learned skill, and it makes a difference in people's lives.*

My brother-in-law Michael shared this story about what it's like to leave a legacy, and it really stuck with me.

He worked at the World Trade Center in New York City during the 9-11 attack, and his office was on the 70th floor. One hundred percent of his team members were able to escape the building successfully. He said it was because one of their team leaders was responsible for fire drills. My brother-in-law said that every time the drill was scheduled, this leader would ensure everybody went through the process of the drill. People would give this leader a hard time, like, "Come on, this an office. What could possibly happen here? Why do I really have to leave my desk? Let's skip this one, it'll be okay." But this leader wasn't having any of it. No excuses. He would make them do the drill no matter what. He would show them where all the exits were, and everyone got out of the building safely on the day of 9-11 because they had been trained by the leader. Everybody got out because he stayed behind to ensure that everybody was out of harm's way. The leader made it out as well, and just a few minutes after he exited, the World Trade Center building collapsed.

# CHAPTER 10:
# YOU CAN DO THIS!

I want to emphasize again that everyone shows up for leadership roles with innate skills that help them succeed.

You already have some skills and traits that are strengths you can leverage. I've saved these for last so you remember them as clearly as possible. There are always going to be gaps and things you need to learn and fill in, but while you're developing those gaps, focus on the strengths you bring that can help you engage your team.

I invite you to take a moment and think about what your friends would say about you. What makes you a great friend can also make you a great leader. What about your co-workers or bosses? What do they notice in you? What traits are you known for in your professional and personal circles? Here is some insight into what your traits say about you:

- Are you a good communicator who is able to inspire and connect people to a vision and use the right words to motivate them to action? You are great at bringing diverse personalities together!

- Are you a quiet type who is a great listener? Do you give other people a chance to talk while you listen with compassion? You build better relationships than talkers do!

- Are you a friendly extrovert who makes friends with everyone? Does your smile warm up the room? People will like you and will want to help and support you!

- Are you a shy introvert who excels at critical thinking and organizing ideas?

- Are you the one who loves nothing more than to be told that something is impossible, then find clever ways to prove them wrong? Your commitment to solutions is a powerful motivator that will spark ideas within the team!

- Do you have sharp organizational skills and an eye for detail? You will keep key systems operating smoothly!

- Are you the "idea person" who has the vision and powerfully inspires people to do what it takes to

achieve the vision, without personally having a clue
how, but trusting in the collective genius?

- Are you the one who loves to make people feel
  welcome, empowered, safe and appreciated? People
  will do whatever you ask if you make them feel like
  they matter!

- Are you a natural diplomat who diffuses emotional
  time bombs with ease, helps people see things from
  another perspective, and helps bridge the gap?

- Do you enjoy nurturing people in their growth and
  helping them become the best version of themselves?

- Are you an eternal optimist who sees problems as
  interesting challenges that can be overcome with a
  little ingenuity?

- Do you have a knack for delivering bad news and
  feedback in a way that empowers people and
  stimulates problem-solving? If so, people will trust
  that you won't blame them for mistakes, but rather
  you will inspire them to work toward a solution.

- Are you the infinitely patient type who doesn't get
  flustered by interpersonal drama?

- In a crisis, are you the type who calmly considers all
  the available data and options before taking action, no
  matter how scared you are?

- Are you the kind of person who is bold and spontaneous (not reckless, but someone who "trusts their training") and inspires others to be bold in their actions as well?

- Do you enjoy solving problems in unexpected ways, "MacGyvering" solutions so out-of-the-box that you're often called "crazy" for your suggestions? Great—that kind of attitude lets people freely share their own out-of-the-box ideas, and often that's the catalyst for great things!

- Do you communicate better in writing where you can carefully measure your words? You have the ability to set detailed expectations, motivate people, outline workflows, and fully express ideas.

The point is you come into this role with unique gifts that can help you become an exceptional leader.

You have the basics, and now it's up to you to take a deep breath, put a big smile on your face, and get to know your people. If ever there was a powerful first step, this is it!

I will never forget those first nights of panic attacks at GE … or at Pepsi. I don't know that the initial new-role fears will ever go away entirely. However, I know how to manage those fears now. I know to "trust my training" and dive right in to getting to know my team and establishing a rapport with them. I know even if *I* don't know what to do, someone on the team will, and likely there will be several individuals I can count on to bring me up to speed. I know if I demonstrate respect, if I show a genuine interest in elevating people by trusting them to bring their own unique backgrounds to the table, ideas will spark. Together we will rise to whatever challenges present themselves, and there is no problem we can't solve.

Being afraid is natural. Team members of the military airborne units whose jobs are to jump out of airplanes have said they know they have a parachute. They have all the training. But still, every time they get ready to jump, they get that rush of fear. But they jump anyway, and that's courage. They let their training kick in.

That's the same thing with leadership. Don't turn away from it because you may be afraid or have some anxiety about it. Trust in the fact that you bring some natural skills and gifts that are going to help you on this journey. The rest of it is to be open to learning, be open to failing, be open to making mistakes, and be open to improving and getting better.

Enjoy the journey and trust me when I tell you that you're going to be much better after you go through it than you would have been had you not taken this path.

Becoming a better leader has been the driving force throughout my career, and I encourage you to experience developing your leadership gifts as well.

Even though I have been a leader for more than 25 years, I continue to learn how to collaborate, delegate, evaluate, bring the right people on board, remove people not productive to the team, resolve conflict, innovate, and support. Becoming more in-tune and engaged has led to my success at General Electric, Pepsi, M&M Mars, and Diageo.

My mission as a leader is to bridge the purpose of the organization to the needs of the people who work there. My leadership success stands on three pillars which provide support to the organization's mission, vision, and values:

- Safety
- Engagement
- Continuous improvement mindset

If you stand true to your commitment to upholding these pillars, you will succeed. You will make a difference in your organization and in the lives of the people who make up your team.

Remember, no matter how uncertain you're feeling as you walk through the door for the first time as a leader, you come into this role with a rich background of skills, knowledge, abilities, experiences, traits, talents, and passions. Therefore, you already possess something you can leverage immediately to help settle you into your new role.

Then, if you focus on connecting with the individuals on your team, ensuring their safety, developing them, and inspiring them, you will create a winning team of engaged, innovative, passionate, and dedicated people. Your team will augment the areas in which you are weak. As a team, you will be unstoppable!

Your status as a leader will make you a member of a broader team. You will have peers or team members that report to your manager as well. Although you and your peers will have separate areas of responsibility, it will be important for you to build a rapport and form alliances with your peer group. Similar to your direct reports, your peers will offer unique perspectives and ideas you can leverage. Partner with your peers to brainstorm ideas on problems within the organization that your areas of responsibility may be faced with. Seek opportunities to exchange ideas on initiatives. Be intentional with your commitment to support one another. By helping each other, you will deliver results and make your manager look good.

While I stated earlier that your learning and development to try to be the best leader you can be will allow you to separate yourself from your peers, it is important that you remember you are not in competition with the peers within your organization. Striving to improve yourself will ensure you are a valuable contributor to the team. Your purpose, however, is to support the growth and improvement of the organization. To do that, you need to work as a team with others within the organization.

You may be asked to contribute to projects or task force teams that are cross-functional teams. This is a great opportunity for you to establish relationships outside of your functional areas. Doing this will allow you to learn about the organization from different perspectives and enable you to provide your team of direct reports with insights they won't have about the organization's journey. Your ability to provide perspective that your direct reports don't have access to will allow you to foster trust as their leader.

As a leader, you will be a member of several teams: your team of direct reports, department teams, and cross-functional teams. The success of any good team depends on how well they are linked to the company's goals and ethics standards (Mission, Vision, and Values) and how well their efforts support the achievement of the goals while upholding ethics. Effective teams and team members must be willing to sacrifice individual achievements in support of the collective achievement. When the team wins, everyone wins.

There is no reason to suffer through the leadership learning curve. Work with a coach who will offer guidance and insight and provide support every step of the way. Linking in with a mentor and a coach will be critical in the early stages of your leadership development. Although you will learn an enormous amount by working with your team of direct reports, they won't and they can't teach you all that you need to learn. Your direct reports can't teach you the correct methods for operating as a leader within the organization. It's important that you have a mentor within the organization who can teach you the culture and best practices that will lead you to the pathway of success. I suggest you look around the organization and align yourself with an experienced leader who you can model and learn from. As you proceed on your journey, you will grow. As you grow, continue to link up with new leaders to provide you with mentorship.

A coach will provide you with a broader perspective on how to improve yourself. Self-improvement will have the greatest impact on your leadership development. A coach will allow you to express concerns regarding challenges on your journey within a safe and confidential environment outside of the company's domain. Working with a coach will provide you with the freedom to think outside the box and challenge the status quo without the risk of judgement. Having the space to do this while partnering with someone who succeeded in this journey will prove to be critical, because it will enable you to share and apply your unique gifts. My coaching services will jump-start your success as a new leader and give you the foundation to help you become extraordinary.

You can do it, but only if you believe it. I can help you believe it.

I can help you engage, lead, and deliver.

- Daryll

P.S. When your leadership responsibility has grown, and you are ready to promote people with potential who may not see themselves as leaders … pass this book on to them!

To sign up for coaching and to participate in Leaders 4 Growth Academy, sign up at www.DKBIndustries.com, www.DKBPartners.com, or www.Leaders4Growth.com.

" *YOUR AUTHENTIC GIFTS*

*ARE ALL YOU NEED*

*TO BE AN*

*OUTSTANDING LEADER.* "

- DARYLL BRYANT

# APPENDIX A

1. Laws of Success, by Napoleon Hill
2. Think and Grow Rich, by Napoleon Hill
3. Psycho-Cybernetics, by Maxwell Maltz
4. How to Win Friends and Influence People, by Dale Carnegie
5. 7 habits of Highly Effective People, by Stephen R. Covey
6. First Break All The Rules: What the World's Greatest Managers Do Differently, by Buckingham, Marcus/ Coffman
7. The Art of War, by Sun Tzu
8. The First 90 Days: Critical Success Strategies for New Leaders at All Levels, by Michael D. Watkins
9. The Power of Positive Thinking, by Norman Vincent Peale
10. TAO TE Ching, by Lao Tzu
11. The Law of Attraction, by Esther Hicks
12. Whale Done: The Power of Positive Relationships, by Kenneth Blanchard Ph.D
13. The Greatest Salesman in the World, by Og Mandino
14. FYI for your Improvement: Competencies Development Guide, by Korn Ferry
15. StrengthsFinder 2.0, by Tom Rath

16. The Unnatural Act of Management, by Everett T Suters

17. Purple Cow: Transform Your Business by Being Remarkable, by Seth Godin

18. Who Moved My Cheese? An Amazing Way to Deal with Change in Your Work and in Your Life, by Spencer Johnson

19. Awaken The Giant Within, by Anthony Robbins

20. Good to Great: Why Some Companies Make the Leap and Others Don't, by Jim Collins

21. Mastery: The Keys to Success and Long-Term Fulfillment, by George Leonard

22. Obvious Adams: The Story of a Successful Businessman, by Robert R. Updegraff

23. Raving Fans, by Ken Blanchard

24. The Richest Man In Babylon, by George Clason

25. Little Black Book of Connections, by Gitomer Jeffrey

26. Building the Bridge As You Walk On It, by Robert Quinn

27. The 48 Laws of Power, by Robert Greene

28. Great Communication Secrets of Great Leaders, by John Baldoni

29. Victory Secrets of Attila the Hun, by Wess Roberts

30. Leadership Secrets of Attila the Hun, by Wess Roberts

31. Jack Straight from the Gut, by Jack Welch

32. Dr. Deming: The American Who Taught the Japanese About Quality, by Rafael Aguayo

33. Getting Past No: Negotiating with Difficult People, by William Ury

34. Lean Thinking, by James P. Womack and Daniel T. Jones

35. What Got You Here Won't Get You There: How Successful People Become Even More Successful, by Marshall Goldsmith

36. The First-Time Manager, by Jim McCormick

37. The Science of Success, by James Arthur Ray

38. The Outliers, by Malcolm Gladwell

39. The Power of Small: Why Little Things Make All the Difference, by Linda Kaplan Thaler

40. The Pursuit of Wow! Every Person's Guide to Topsy-Turvy Times, by Tom Peters

41. Beware of the Naked Man Who Offers You His Shirt, by Harvey Mackay

42. Control Your Destiny or Someone Else Will, by Noel M. Tichy

43. Chicken Soup for the Soul, by Jack Canfield

44. Your Greatest Power, by Martin Kohe

45. Movies to Manage By, by John Clemens

46. The Speed of Trust, by Stephen M. Covey

47. The 5 Dysfunctions of a Team, by Patrick Lencioni
48. Taking People With You, by David Novak
49. Mindfulness: A Practical Guide, by Tessa Watt
50. The Exceptional Presenter: A Proven Formula to Open Up and Own the Room, by Timothy J Koegel
51. The Conquest of Happiness, by Bertrand Russell
52. 7 Spiritual Laws of Success, by Deepak Chopra
53. Self Mastery Through Conscious Autosuggestion and The Practice of Autosuggestion, by Emile Cou
54. The Game of Work, by Charles Coonradt
55. HBR's 10 Must Reads on Managing Yourself, by Harvard Business Review
56. Nuts!: Southwest Airlines Crazy Recipe for Business and Success, by Kevin Freiberg
57. Customer Satisfaction is Worthless, Customer Loyalty is Priceless: How to Make Customers Love You, Keep Them Coming Back and Tell Everyone They Know, by Jeffrey Gitomer
58. Execution: The Discipline of Getting Things Done, by Larry Bossidy
59. The Checklist Manifesto: How to Get Things Right, by Atul Gawande
60. The Spirit to Serve Marriott's Way, by J.W. Marriott

# BIBLIOGRAPHY

1. Jim Harter and Amy Adkins, "Employees Want a Lot More From Their Managers," *Gallup Workplace*, 8 Apr 2015.

2. Jennifer Reingold, "How a Radical Shift Left Zappos Reeling," *Fortune*, 4 Mar 2016.

3. Zlati Meyer, "After Chipotle's queso-gate and food safety issues, can a new CEO help?" *USA Today*, 29 Dec 2017.

4. Chase Purdy, "Wracked with troubles, Chipotle has a new leader and a mission to prepare 'better food'," *Quartz*, 12 Dec 2016.

5. Emma Woollacott, "Lessons from history's worst CEOs," *CEO Magazine*, 18 July 2018.

6. Chunka Mui, "The Lesson That Market Leaders Are Failing To Learn From Xerox PARC," *Forbes*, 1 Aug 2012.

7. Drake Baer, "How Changing One Habit Helped Quintuple Alcoa's Income," *Business Insider*, 9 Apr 2014.

8. Paul O'Neil (CEO of Alcoa), "It's All About Safety," *YouTube*, 12 June 2015, viewed on 18 Dec 2018.

# ABOUT THE AUTHOR

Daryll Bryant is a transformational leader who has a passion for creating engaging work environments that are great places to work and produce phenomenal results. Daryll has a distinguished career in manufacturing where he held frontline, mid-management, and executive leadership roles, providing proven results for respectable Fortune 100 organizations such as Pepsi, M&M Mars, GE, and DIAGEO Wine & Spirits. He has a vast repository of high-level skill sets as an engineer, change leader, and lean practitioner.

Daryll's business acumen is best displayed by his exceptional talent as a turnaround expert in business operations. He has a unique ability to engage staff at every level of the organization to take ownership and drive improvements, resulting in consistent annual cost savings, profit increases, improved employee morale, and a results-oriented organizational culture.

Daryll's 25 years of business leadership experience has led him to develop DKB Consulting Partners and a Leadership Academy (Leaders 4 Growth Academy). "One way we will get Americans back to work is by making things again and developing leaders who can unlock the collective genius of their people," he passionately pleas. His bold vision is to provide leadership coaching and development to "New Leaders" with less than five years of leadership experience. The Mission of Leaders 4 Growth Academy is to remove the mystery from the role of leader by providing tools, techniques, and global best practices to New Leaders that will enable them to have success in their roles. Leaders 4 Growth Academy's purpose is to help aspiring leaders become authentic leaders by teaching them to identify and leverage their unique gifts they can use to begin their leadership journey.

Daryll sees no contradiction in business success and being a committed husband and father of three. He regards business and family success as complimentary. Civic-minded, he constantly seeks opportunities to improve communities in which he resides and serves on a number of non-profit and civic boards.

To Contact DKB Consulting Partners or Leaders 4 Growth Academy, go to www.DKBIndustries.com, www.DKBPartners.com, or www.Leaders4Growth.com.

Made in the USA
Middletown, DE
16 September 2023